TABLE OF CONTENTS

W9-AUI-323

━━━━►⧨◄━━━━

A special thanks to my sister, Flo Warriner, for her editorial assistance.

━━━━►⧨◄━━━━

Unless otherwise indicated, all Scripture quotations are taken from the King James Version of the Bible.

The Uncommon Dream · ISBN 1-56394-124-4 /B-135

Publisher/Editor: Deborah Murdock Johnson
Published by The Wisdom Center · 4051 Denton Hwy. · Ft. Worth, Texas 76117
1-817-759-BOOK · 1-817-759-0300
You Will Love Our Website...! www.TheWisdomCenter.tv

Accuracy Department: To our Friends and Partners...We welcome any comments on errors or misprints you find in our book...Email our department: AccuracyDept@thewisdomcenter.tv. Your aid in helping us excel is highly valued.

An Uncommon Dream
Requires
Uncommon Faith.

-MIKE MURDOCK

WHY I WROTE THIS BOOK

Pain Is Everywhere.

I just flew in late last night from Virginia, meeting with a small inner circle of my strongest Partners.

Hour after hour, I saw tear-drenched faces and looked at the photographs of rebellious children, held business cards in my hand, praying for the Birthing and Miracle of Unfulfilled Dreams.

Your Uncommon Dream matters to me.

Your are my Assignment. I breathe it. I live it. I long to unleash the unused, unfocused FAITH in you...that will...Move Your Mountain.

That's Why I Wrote This Book.

Mike Murdock

P. S. Who is *Your* Assignment? I hope you will invest in an extra copy of this book for the person who matters most to you.

The Uncommon Dream
    Must Be Born Within You
And Not Borrowed
    From Someone Else.

-MIKE MURDOCK

1

THE UNCOMMON DREAM IS THE INNER MIND PICTURE YOU HAVE OF THE FUTURE YOU DESIRE

Your Mind Is Your Personal World.
The pictures in your mind are controlling your life. This explains the Seed-Pictures God plants inside your mind. Photographs of what you can achieve... become...do...have.

You choose your reaction to every mind picture. You can believe it. Grow it. Feed it. Protect it. Build your life around it. Doubt it...and *it will die.*

The Uncommon Dream is not always The Divine *Prediction.* It is simply the mental picture of something you desire. The Uncommon Dream is The Divine *Possibility.*

What is **The Uncommon Dream...for You?** It is the Divine Photograph of You in Your Future.

Joseph experienced it...and it swept him, like a current, from the prison to the palace. It will require every *gift* within you.

▶ The Uncommon Dream Is *Attainable.*

▶ The Uncommon Dream Is *Closer* Than

You Can Imagine.
▶ The Uncommon Dream Will Be Your *Distinction*.
▶ The Uncommon Dream Can Come *True*.

That is why this book can change your life.

▶ Dreamers are often vulnerable to disappointment.
▶ Dreamers feel alone.
▶ Dreamers often hurt deeply inside.
▶ Dreamers are often misunderstood.

Your *Moment* will come.

Your *Hour* will arrive.

▶ Your *Future* will ignite.

The Uncommon Dream Is Your...

▶ *Difference* From Others.
▶ *Entry* Into Significance.
▶ *Compass* In Your Life.
▶ *Invisible* Companion.
▶ *Master Key*...To Hidden Treasures.

The Uncommon Dream Is The Inner Mind Picture Of The Future You Desire.

RECOMMENDED FOR YOUR WISDOM LIBRARY:
B-08 Enjoying the Winning Life (32 pages/$3)
B-11 Dream Seeds (106 pages/$9)

2

THE UNCOMMON DREAM WILL BIRTH THE UNCOMMON LIFE

Never Trivialize Your Inner Dreams.

Journal your Dreams...even in the midnight hour...*fragmented* dreams...*odd* dreams...*weird* dreams...*strange* dreams are even worthy of documentation.

Often, we speak laughingly and dismissively of our friends night dreams as, "you ate too much pizza... you should not have taken that Nyquil."

Whether You Experience The Night Dreams During Your Sleep Or Mind-Dream During The Day Of Something You Want In Your Future... *Your Imagined Dreams Have Great Power.*

God Will Use Dreams To Talk To You.

When God talks to *families*...He talks through the *children*.

When God talks to *nations*...He talks through the *economy*.

God uses Dreams for your *protection*...similar to when the life of Jesus was being protected.

God even gives Dreams to *evil* men... Pharaoh... Nebuchadnezzar...*to warn or document divine mercy.*

Your *responsibility is to interpret the Dream accurately.* If you cannot find the answer...at least document it until someone is able to help you interpret the Dream.

Avoid trivializing even your night dreams.

Dreams may *encourage* or *motivate* you to intercede for someone...to become more *attentive to a parent*.

God wants you to record your dreams... document the *Night* Dream.

Your Mind-Dream Is Different Than Your Night Dream. We use this same phraseology when we talk about an *invisible* picture of a future we desire.

- ► *What is the Picture you have of your future?*
- ► *What is your Dream for a new house?*
- ► *What is your Dream for starting a business?*
- ► *What are your Dreams for your children?*
- ► *What is your most Dominant Dream this very moment?*
- ► *Are you willing to devote all your time and attention to it?*
- ► *Are you willing to create a plan that will make it happen?*

4 Expectations Of The Uncommon Dream

1. *The Uncommon Dream May Appear Impossible.*

2. *The Uncommon Dream Is What You Want To Be, Do Or Have.*

3. *The Uncommon Dream Will Energize You To Leave The Present And Enter Your Future.*

4. *An Uncommon Future Will Require Uncommon Preparation.* You see, the most wonderful thing that can happen to a Dream is a *specific plan of*

action.

Planning Always Produces Self-Confidence. It is one of the Golden Secrets of the Uncommon Dreamer.

Reassess and re-evaluate your personal goals.

The greatest goal in my life today is staying in The Secret Place of prayer and writing what The Holy Spirit teaches me through His Word and daily experiences.

20 Keys To Unleashing Your Uncommon Dream

1. Invest One Hour In Writing Down Clearly The Goals That Really Matter To You At This Point. Keep this list confidential and private. "Write the vision, and make it plain upon tables, that he may run that readeth it," (Habakkuk 2:2).

2. Permit Unexciting Dreams Of Yesterday To Die. Stop pursuing yesterday goals that no longer excite you. Do not feel obligated to keep trying to obtain them...if you no longer have a true passion for them. (See Isaiah 43:18-19.)

3. Do Not Depend On Others To Understand Your Dreams And Goals. Permit them freedom for their chosen focus, also. They have every right to choose what they love. Refuse to be intimidated by their efforts to persuade you to move in a different direction with your life.

4. Never Make Permanent Decisions Because Of Temporary Feelings. One young woman got so excited about a new friend; she dropped the lease on her own apartment and moved into the apartment of her new friend. Within a week, she realized she had made a mistake. They were not compatible in a close environment. *Time Will Expose What Interrogation Cannot.*

5. Avoid Intimate Relationships With Those Who Do Not Really Respect Your Dreams. You will have to sever ties. *Wrong people do not always leave your life voluntarily.* Life is too short to permit discouragers close to you. "And have no fellowship with the unfruitful works of darkness, but rather reprove them," (Ephesians 5:11). *Those Who Disagree With Your Goals Will Usually Disagree With Your Decisions.*

6. Anticipate Changes In Your Needs And Goals. Your present feelings and opinions are rarely permanent. New experiences are coming. New relationships are ahead.

When you *assess* and *evaluate* your goals, you will unclutter your life of the unnecessary. *Prioritize* your most important goals.

7. Nobody Can Determine Your Own Goals For You. You must decide what generates joy in your own heart. *Your Focus Decides Your Feelings.*

8. Different People Have Different Goals. What is important to me may be very unimportant to another. When others come in my presence, our *differences emerge.*

One of my personal goals involves a Wisdom Mentorship Program for Families. It will be a 10-year Mentorship Program For Parents...consisting of 120 Wisdom books. (There will be a chapter for each day of the month.) This will be a Mentorship System for parents to use with their children ages six to sixteen. This provides parents with a "Wisdom Encyclopedia" for their family.

Imagine this incredible picture! Begin each

morning during breakfast...reading one chapter and mentoring your children on such topics as: 31 Facts about God, 31 Facts about Jesus, 31 Facts about The Holy Spirit, and other powerful, *life-changing* themes.

You, too, can develop your own Focus and Plan for your life.

9. Do Not Wait For Others To Inspire You Regarding Your Dreams. Your friends may distract you and not have the same values you are pursuing.

Accept their different values. *The Difference In People Is The Future They Are Pursuing.*

10. You Must Determine What Your Goals Are Financially, Spiritually Or Physically. Others cannot borrow your goals. You may have wonderful goals for those you love, but if they do not have the same Dream for themselves *it is a waste of your time and energy.*

Some years ago, I purchased a special building for a physical fitness center for my staff. I was so excited. I hired a trainer to assist each of my staff in developing their maximum level of health. The excitement lasted one month.

At the end of three weeks, only two people would show up at the special meeting with the trainer that was costing me $75 an hour. Although the fee for the trainer had been paid for them, they simply did not have any *personal* fitness goals.

My *investment* was wasted. You cannot attempt to control the lives of others.

11. Avoid Intimate Relationships With People Who Disrespect Your Dreams. Yes, you may minister to them in the crisis moments of their lives. You can encourage and speak words that will strengthen and bless them. *Access Is First A Gift,*

Then A Test, Then A Reward.
> ▶ *Intimacy* should be earned.
> ▶ *Access* should be a privilege.
> ▶ *Relationship* should be a reward for *respect.*

12. Place Pictures Of Your Goals And Dreams On The Walls Of Your Home And Office. For example, if you have a Dream of losing weight, place pictures that *inspire you* and excite you to lose those unwanted pounds.

Do you have a Dream of owning your own home? What you keep looking at *continuously* will influence your conversation and your faith. *What You See Determines What You Desire.*

13. Write Out Your Dream On Paper. "Write the vision, and make it plain upon tables, that he may run that readeth it," (Habakkuk 2:2).

Some do not make plans because they simply have never been taught how to create a plan.

14. Write Your Personal Definition Of Success. Document the most *specific, clear and simple definition* of what you want to accomplish.

15. Write Down Five Reasons You Want To Succeed. Keep a list of those you love who will succeed *because of your fulfilled Dream.* This is very important. Their countenance and their own joy will motivate you during difficult days.

16. Write Down Every Detail Involved In Achieving Your Dream. Every *step*...every *detail* you can think of. It might be easier to dictate. It is proven we talk six times faster than we write.

17. Write Down Every Question You Should Be Asking. Solutions will be birthed the moment you focus on the quality of your questions. *The Quality Of*

Your Questions Will Determine The Quality Of Your Answers.

18. Write Down The Names Of Those Who Can Participate In Your Dream. Write at the top of the page, "My Circle of Counsel for My Dream." This will be those who brainstorm and provide feedback and advice regarding your Dream. Accepting the help and gifts of others in your life will accelerate your achievements.

Stay in the center of your own expertise. Do not attempt to be an expert in everything. I have made this mistake. Rather than hire experts, I have the tendency to want to learn about everything. That will slow you down.

*Avoid focusing only on learning...*strive for completion of your goals.

Focus your time and energy on a single Dream or Goal. *You Will Only Have Significant Success With Something That Is An Obsession.*

19. Respect And Reward Every Relationship Committed To Birthing The Uncommon Dream Of Your Life. It guarantees satisfaction.

20. Learn To Generate Excitement In Others To Get Them Involved With The Uncommon Dream.

The Uncommon Dream Will Birth The Uncommon Life.

RECOMMENDED FOR YOUR WISDOM LIBRARY:

B-114   The Law of Recognition (247 pages/$10)
TS-01   Wisdom for Winning (6 tapes/$30)
TS-07   Secrets of the Greatest Achievers Who Ever Lived, Series 2 (6 tapes/$30)

Your Significance Is Not In
  Your Similarity To Another,
But In Your Point Of Difference
    From Another.

-MIKE MURDOCK

❧ 3 ❧

THE UNCOMMON DREAM WILL REQUIRE UNCOMMON SELF-CONFIDENCE

Self-Confidence Is Magnetic.

Thoughts have a presence. Whatever you are thinking about will influence the atmosphere around you. It stirs the heart of those who do not have self-confidence. It creates a desire in others...*they want to be in your presence.*

3 Keys To Self-Confidence

1. **Know Your Assignment.** You were created to solve a problem. Discover what it is.

Your *Assignment* is any problem you were created to solve while you are here on earth. You must be persuaded you are truly in the center of where you belong.

2. **Know Your Dominant Gift.** It could be organization, computers, administration or communication. Knowing your *difference* from others will birth remarkable inner peace. *Your Significance Is Not In Your Similarity To Another, But In Your Point Of Difference From Another.*

3. **Identify Your Persuasions.** When I walk to the pulpit or platform to speak, I never lack

confidence. I feel that I know my subject more than anyone present does! It is why I am there. I stay in the center of my Belief System.

Exploration and experimenting is different than my core *confidence* in my beliefs.

You have to know more about your chosen subject than others around you do...*to generate confidence. Information Births Confidence.*

7 Steps That Can Unlock Your Self-Confidence

1.   Recognize That Your Creator Wants Good Things For You. "Every good gift and every perfect gift is from above, and cometh down from the Father of lights, with whom is no variableness, neither shadow of turning," (James 1:17).

2.   Verify That Your Dream Is Not Contrary To The Laws Of God Or Man. Avoid anything that condemns your inner invisible referee...*your conscience.* Your conscience must be at peace for your greatest ideas to emerge. You must not attempt to pursue anything that troubles your *heart, soul* and *mind. The Seeds Of Greatness Grow Best In The Soil Of Peace.*

3.   Fill Every Conversation With Faith-Talk About Your Dream. *Words matter.* They move you toward your Dream or away from it. Your words should *continuously* reflect hope in your future. When someone speaks to you with doubt and unbelief, *boldly refute those words.* Do not receive them. *Replace their evil report with your own good report.*

Inform others of the great things that are

happening in your life. Remember, your faith is like a muscle that grows and becomes strong through *continuous* use. *Your Words Are The Seeds For Feelings.*

4. Pursue Access Of Those Whose Fire Burns Brighter Than Your Own. Who are the most successful people you presently know?

Who are the people who have succeeded in the same arena in which you desire to succeed?

Schedule appointments with them...a special lunch. *Interrogate, interview* and *receive* the information they have.

Do not feel obligated to tell them all of your plans. *Respect and humbly pursue their advice and counsel.* Let them light your fire as often as possible.

Every Friendship Nurtures A Strength Or A Weakness.

5. Remember That Your Own Dream Is A Special Seed You Are Sowing Into The Hearts Of Others. Sometimes, they are excited and thrilled with you. However, there will be times when those closest to you are not ready to receive what you want to share.

A farmer knows his field requires preparation before he plants his seed. Likewise, the minds and hearts of those you love may require preparation as well. *Be patient.*

6. Remember That Your Dream May Intimidate Those Close To You And Make Them Feel Uncomfortable. It is important to remember that your Dream is yours alone. Others do not *feel* what you feel, *see* what you see, or *know* what you know. *How can they understand your joy when they* *have not lived with your sorrow?*

Those closest to you may *misread* you or even *misjudge* you because they feel uncomfortable. Forcing them to respond to your Dream, and your enthusiasm may be intimidating.

Perhaps, they are "*unstretched.*" You are excited about success, while they are hoping only to *survive.*

7. Keep Your Fire Fueled. Fertilize your own dreams. *Talk* about them. Build on them. You cannot expect to light someone else's fire until you have lit the fire *within yourself.*

Desire Is The Greatest Seed You Could Possess. You are reading this book. It is proof of your *desire*...your *need*...to *succeed. Fuel this obsession.*

- ▶ Desire Determines What You *Learn.*
- ▶ Desire Determines What You *Pursue.*
- ▶ Desire Creates *Endurance* And *Strength.*
- ▶ Desire Separates You From The *Common* Person.
- ▶ Desire Makes It Possible To *Leave* Egypt...And *Move* Toward Canaan.

4 Kinds Of People Who Always Fail

1. **The *Undecided.***
2. **The *Unlearned.***
3. **The *Unfocused.***
4. **The *Unexcited.***

The saddest tragedy of life is a heart that has not caught fire. The mind of such a person is like a huge field into which no Seed has been sown. *Nothing of worth is growing.*

This person will not produce *greatness, miracles*

or an *uncommon* life.

You must recognize this tragedy. Stay *focused*, *enthusiastic* and *aggressively* happy.

4 Keys To Unleashing The Uncommon Dream

1. Decide What Your Uncommon Dream Really Is.

2. Develop The Magnet Within You... Toward Your Dream.

3. Discern The Circle Of Counsel To Help Achieve Your Dream.

4. Invest Time In Creating A Dream Wall... Pictures Of Your Dream.

The Uncommon Dream Will Require Uncommon Self-Confidence.

The Battle Of Your Life Is
For Your Mind.
The Battle Of The Mind Is
For Focus.

-MIKE MURDOCK

 4

THE UNCOMMON DREAM DESERVES YOUR TOTAL FOCUS

The Battle Of Your Life Is For Your Mind.
The Battle Of The Mind Is For Focus.
The Uncommon Dream Must Qualify For Your Undivided Focus.

Your Health Affects Your Focus

Rest Produces Hope. When you are mentally at rest, your mind moves to *positive* things, *wonderful* and *glorious* dreams...things you want to do and accomplish.

When you are weary, you are not the same person. You do not have the same kind of *faith... enthusiasm* or *patience*.

When you are *rested, strengthened* and *well* in your spirit...*your faith is renewed. Your Focus Decides Your Feelings.*

Fatigue Can Become Deadly. When you are tired at night, things that would normally seem simple...suddenly feel very burdensome and complex to you.

Tasks that usually take minimal effort suddenly seem too much to complete. You may even blame others when things go wrong.

Faith does not always flow easily through a tired body. *Tired Eyes Rarely See A Great Future.*

Fatigue Is An Enemy To Your Focus. Many have failed because of exhaustion, over-scheduling and attempting too many tasks in a day.

The famed billionaire, J. Paul Getty once said, "I have seen as many people fail from attempting too many things as those who attempt too little."

11 Mistakes Fatigue Will Create

1. Fatigue Makes Mountains You Are Facing...Appear Bigger.

2. Fatigue Causes Valleys You Are Experiencing...Appear Deeper.

3. Fatigue Magnifies The Pain Of Offenses.

4. Fatigue Births Impatience...With Those You Work Around.

5. Fatigue Creates An Obsession With Immediate Results Instead Of The Protocol For Achieving Them.

6. Fatigue Turns Your Focus To Short-Term Goals Rather Than Long-Term Goals.

7. Fatigue Dissolves Constraints, Unleashing Destructive Words.

8. Fatigue Makes You Unwilling To Invest Time To Plan Ahead.

9. Fatigue Creates Self-Absorption And Meditation On Your Own Mistakes.

10. Fatigue Magnifies The Flaws In Those You Love.

11. Fatigue Weakens Your Courage To Pursue Worthwhile Dreams.

Remember Wisdom Key #96: *When Fatigue Walks In, Faith Walks Out.* Never make important decisions unless you are strengthened, mentally alert and spiritually perceptive.

The Uncommon Dream can be renewed when your body is renewed physically and mentally.

Remember Wisdom Key #157: *The Only Reason Men Fail Is Broken Focus.* You can only succeed at something that consumes you. Your Uncommon Dream will require all of you...your *time, your energy and your relationships.*

15 Rewards Of Focus

1. *Focus Enables You To Find The Shortest Road To Your Destination.* It is the secret of the martial arts...the laser beam...and uncommon achievements.

2. *Focus Will Expose The Unqualified In Your Life.* When you decide to do right...wrong people will want to leave your life.

3. *Focus Forces Adversaries To Become Exposed.* Your chosen focus is the world you have created for your mind.

4. *Your Focus Decides Your Personal Reaction Of Yourself And Others.*

When *Jesus* began to talk about His deity, His enemies reacted with intense anger and hatred.

When *Moses* focused on the exodus of the Israelites from Egypt, Pharaoh brought his best efforts forward to prevent it.

When the *blind man* focused on crying out to Jesus, those around him told him to "be quiet."

5. *Your Focus Distinguishes You From Others.* Distinguish between what is important and what is less important. Everything *appears* important. Identify the difference...between what is and what is not top priority—*tasks...friendships...values.*

Permit others to do their jobs. Stay in the center of your own Assignment. Do not attempt to solve the problems assigned to others.

6. *Your Focus Will Increase Your Passion.*

7. *Your Focus Will Unleash New Creativity.*

8. *Your Focus Will Expose What Is Unnecessary.*

9. *Your Focus Will Identify Passive, Uncaring People In Your Life.*

10. *Your Focus Will Reveal Distractions.*

11. *Your Focus Increases Your Determination.*

12. *Your Focus Simplifies Your Day.*

13. *Your Focus Decides Who Qualifies For Access.*

14. *Your Focus Rewrites Every Conversation.*

15. *Your Focus Discourages Parasites Who Linger Around You.*

Keep Focusing On Your Dream!

▶ Your Dream *will require time for gathering data and important information.*

▶ Your Dream *will require time for developing an understanding, education and knowledge.*

▶ Your Dream *must be worthy of your focus, attention and time.* If you do not think so, you will not empty your life into it.

You must find something that will challenge you...something worth depositing your life into. You cannot make some decisions without investing a proper amount of time.

Great achievements in life require time.

Great relationships require quality time.

Skyscrapers require more construction time than the small log cabin.

A Rolls Royce automobile is costlier than a bike.

Is your present receiving your total *focus, attention and creativity?* Do you daydream about being somewhere else? You will never know how successful you can truly become until your Dream receives every part of you.

The Uncommon Dream Deserves Your Total Focus.

The Clearer Your Goals,
    The Greater Your Faith.

-MIKE MURDOCK

≈ 5 ≈

THE UNCOMMON DREAM WILL REQUIRE A DETAILED PLAN

━━━▶◦◦◦◀━━━

A Plan Is A Written Map To Your Goal.

God is a Planner. Anyone who schedules supper 6,000 years in advance...is a *Master* Organizer.

The Uncommon Dream will take a gigantic leap forward once you invest your time in a detailed plan. Details increase your confidence.

God Commended Ants For Their Planning. "Go to the ant, thou sluggard; consider her ways, and be wise: which having no guide, overseer, or ruler, Provideth her meat in the summer, and gathereth her food in the harvest," (Proverbs 6:6-8).

Doubters Can Become Believers...When They See The Plan.

Plans require time. They are laborious...not always easy.

▶ *Anything You Can See Becomes Believable.*

▶ *Anything Believable Becomes Achievable.*

Years ago, I had a product that would greatly bless a religious organization. I met with twelve of their board members.

The least wealthy of the board members had a net worth of $40 million. I showed how my product would increase a profit of $25 million for their company. At the beginning, they said it would take several weeks before they could accept my product.

I decided to invest $850 in developing a visual flip chart...*a plan* to *show them what I could see in my mind.* When you take time to write out a clear plan... others see your plan, and have the confidence to get involved.

They decided that night to adopt the plan. Later, some complications arose and the organization divided. But I discovered that *persuasion is in clarity. When Others See What You Are Seeing, They Will Feel What You Are Feeling.*

Failure To Plan Will Derail Your Dream

Your life is like the *Golden Train of Success on the Track of Success,* and God schedules *Cities of Accomplishments* in your future.

Every morning, God gives you 24 Golden *Boxcars.* What you schedule in those 24 Golden *Hours,* determines the speed and the distance your train will move.

If you do not plan what goes in those 24 hours... those 24 Golden Boxcars, somebody else is going to fill them for you with their own set of tasks.

Have you ever had somebody come in and dump into your 24 Golden Boxcars? Have you ever had your train derailed for a day?

It happens when you fail to schedule your day. Remember Wisdom Key #230: Yesterday Is In The Tomb; Tomorrow Is In The Womb. The Only Place You Will Ever Be Is Today.

If you cannot make 24 hours go right, how can you

make 24 years go right? If you cannot make one day go in the right direction, how are you going to make your whole life go right?

Few understand planning. Planning is extremely difficult. It requires walking away from *secondary* desires.

A Plan Is A Written Map From Your Present To Your Future

Noah had a plan for the *Ark.*
Moses had a plan for the *Tabernacle.*
Solomon had a plan for the *Temple.*
Solomon was an Uncommon Dreamer and meticulous planner. He created a $500 billion temple.

When God begins to deal with your life...He will have a plan. It takes a *moment* to hear a divine command. It takes your *lifetime* to discern the plan.

► *There Is A Plan.*
► *There Is A Place He Wants You To Be.*
► *There Is A Time He Wants You To Be There.*
► *There Are People Destined For Your Life To Participate In Your Dream.*

Picture...*Visualize* your Dream.

Plan Your Day Around The Uncommon Dream

When you plan your day, you are planning your life. Every morning write down 7 tasks you will do that day. Attach each of those 7 tasks to a time frame. *God is very time-conscious. You also must become time-conscious.*

Write down 7 daily goals. Keep it simple.

1. 7:00 - Read my Bible.
2. 7:30 - Get dressed.
3. 9:00 - Clean my room.

All People Who Have Great Dreams And Goals...Have Detailed Plans. All the multi-millionaires that you hear about have plans that you would not believe. Their plans are listed...they are *written.* They have staff to assist them to do nothing but layout maps for their life...*and they do accomplish their dreams.*

This is what we want to help you do...*develop a map for your life.*

Where do you want to be in 1 year, 5 years, 10 years and 20 years; should Jesus tarry? You must have a plan to work with. You can always *change it, alter it, add to it or delete it.*

A Dream must be so big that it enters every conversation and anything else discussed becomes boring to you. *Your Whole Worth In Life Links To The Problems You Are Willing To Solve.*

What Is The Greatest Dream In Your Heart? When I say, Bill Gates, you know he is all about... *Computers.* Evander Holyfield...*Boxing.* Thomas Edison...*Inventions.* Benny Hinn...*Healing.* Billy Graham...*Salvation.*

If I say your name and you cannot tell me in one single sentence what your Dream is...*you do not yet know what your Dream is.*

If you do not know your Dream, nobody else knows it, which means...nobody will participate in it. Your Dream must consume you. Remember Wisdom Key #290: *You Will Only Have Significant Success With Something That Is An Obsession.*

Anticipate Demonic Distractions

Satan Never Reacts To Your Past. He Reacts To Your Future. The abortion issue is greater than a murder issue. It is a satanic strategy to stop the entry of deliverers into a generation. He tried it with Jesus. He tried it with Moses...and he will try it with you.

Take time to build your Dream on God's schedule. There are two ways to get out of God's will...*to move ahead or lag behind.*

In The Secret Place, you must listen for *directions* and timing to achieve anything with God's approval. Stay in His presence *long enough...*then you will discover His Plan.

Remember Wisdom Key #43: *One Hour In The Presence Of God Will Reveal The Flaws Of Your Most Carefully Laid Plans.*

The Bible Is A Collection Of God's Plans. "For which of you, intending to build a tower, sitteth not down first, and counteth the cost, whether he have sufficient to finish it?" (Luke 14:28).

A *thought* is not a plan.

A *wish* is not a plan.

A *possibility* is not a plan.

True champions invest time and energy to develop a clear-cut goal and Dream. They plan for their life.

The entire universe reveals planning...*by a Divine Force.* It is said that if we were a few miles closer to the sun, we would burn up. If we were a few miles farther away from the sun, we would freeze to death.

God is a *strategist...*an *organizer...*an *administrator.* God plans. He is not *temperamental, moody* or *erratic* in His design.

God Respects Men Who Plan. God respects men who believe in their Dream enough to labor over a plan.

Solomon's 17 Secrets
For Achieving Your Dream

1. He Established A Clear-Cut Goal. (See 2 Chronicles 2:1.)

2. He Received God's Approval For His Project. (See 2 Chronicles 7:16.)

3. He Announced The Goal And Explained Its Value And Purpose. (See 2 Chronicles 2:3-4.)

4. He Valued The Greatness Of His Goal And Was Proud Of It. (See 2 Chronicles 2:5.)

5. He Developed A Detailed Plan. (See 2 Chronicles 3:3-5.)

6. He Acknowledged His Limitations. (See 2 Chronicles 2:6.)

7. He Established A Reputation Of Integrity. (See 2 Chronicles 2:11-12.)

8. He Consulted Other Achievers Related To His Project. (See 2 Chronicles 2:3.)

9. He Acknowledged Past Favors And Asked For Assistance. (See 2 Chronicles 2:3.)

10. He Set A First-Class Level Of Quality. (See 2 Chronicles 3:6-7.)

11. He Involved As Many People As Possible In The Project. (See 2 Chronicles 2:17-18.)

12. He Organized And Delegated Responsibilities. (See 2 Chronicles 2:18.)

13. He Used The Expertise Of Specialists. (See 2 Chronicles 2:7, 14.)

14. He Made The Description And Details Of All Contracts Clear. (See 2 Chronicles 2:10.)

15. He Compensated And Rewarded Those Who Assisted Him In Achieving His Goal. (See 2 Chronicles 2:9.)

16. He Kept Alive The Enthusiasm And Greatness Of His Project. (See 2 Chronicles 2:9.)

17. He Established A Production Schedule. (See 2 Chronicles 3:2; 5:1.)

Your future is whatever you decide you want it to be. An evil man with a plan for his future will achieve it before a Christian without a plan.

God works...*by His Laws.*

Trusting His laws...*is trusting Him.*

When you trust the instructor...you trust the instruction. The proof that you trust the instructor is your *reaction* to his instructions.

The Uncommon Dream Will Require A Detailed Plan Followed Carefully.

An Uncommon Dream
Requires
Uncommon Preparation.

-MIKE MURDOCK

❧ 6 ❧

THE UNCOMMON DREAM WILL REQUIRE UNCOMMON PREPARATION

Your Future Has A Price...Preparation.

Preparation Is The Seed For Uncommon Achievement.

God even uses night dreams to prepare for bad times as he did to Joseph who enabled Pharaoh to prepare for 7 years of famine.

The purpose of the prosperity message is not excess but preparation when famine comes, and God's people can be sustained.

The purpose of the prosperity message is not to buy Rolls Royces, diamond rings, or clothes.

The Divine purpose for prosperity is to continue provision during difficult times. A Dream is partially for preparation. It is not a prediction in every case. There is truth in the phrase, "short-time pain for long-time gain."

Jesus prepared thirty years...for three-and-a-half years of ministry.

Moses prepared eighty years...to become the deliverer for the Israelites.

Successful books require years of research and gathering of data and knowledge.

Someone told me that the height of a tree was equal to the length of the root beneath the soil.

The *taller* the tree...*the longer the roots.* The *stronger* the tree *determines* the number of years.

The Quality Of Your Preparation Will Determine The Quality Of Your Future.

8 Rewards Of Preparation

1.   Remember The Scriptural Guarantee Of Harvest. "And let us not be weary in well doing: for in due season we shall reap, if we faint not," (Galatians 6:9). That is the guarantee of Jesus to you. *Reaping is inevitable to those who are patient.* "The Lord is good unto them that wait for Him," (Lamentations 3:25).

2.   Preparation Is Not Loss Of Time But A Seed And Investment. *Great dreams involve time.* The Uncommon Dream will require wise management of your time. Become *time-conscious.* Make *every* hour count.

3.   Becoming Skilled In Your Present Position Is Part Of Your Divine Preparation. Joseph believed this. The Dream of Pharaoh was not the first Dream Joseph interpreted accurately. He simply collected another *Success Memory* when he interpreted the dreams of the butler and the baker.

4.   Preparation Increases Your Self-Confidence.

5.   Preparation Is The Catalyst For Valuable Relationships.

6.   Preparation Focuses Your Total Attention On The People That Are Necessary To Achieve Your Goal.

7. **Preparation Reveals The Available Time You Have To Achieve Your Goal And The Financial Cost Involved.**

8. **Preparation Will Reveal The Shortest Route To Your Goal.**

The Future Has A Price...

...The Price Is To Let Go Of Yesterday.

...The Price Of Canaan Is The Exit From Egypt.

You cannot enter the future until you relinquish the past.

You cannot qualify for tomorrow until you are willing to let go of the comfort today.

You have no authorization for the palace in your future if you are unwilling to learn protocol for entry and remaining.

The Entire Bible Is About Preparation.

The story of Esther is a story of preparation... soaking twelve months in oil...before she could spend one night with the king. (See Esther Chapter 2.)

The story of Ruth is about preparation in the fields of Boaz. Ruth was becoming familiar with the vocabulary of the servants so she could learn to converse with Boaz. *Something In Your Present Is Necessary To Qualify You For Your Future.*

The Uncommon Dream Will Require Uncommon Preparation To Succeed.

The Uncommon Dream
Is An Effective Rival
To Every Distraction
And Adversary.

-MIKE MURDOCK

≈ 7 ≈

THE UNCOMMON DREAM WILL UNLEASH AN UNCOMMON ENEMY

Anything God Loves...Hell Hates.

A Dream From God Will Activate The Enemies Of God. An Uncommon Dream will activate Uncommon *Adversity...*Uncommon *Enemies.*

When Satan Wants To Destroy You, He Puts A Person Into Your Life (Wisdom Key #215).

Remember Wisdom Key #117: *An Uncontested Enemy Will Flourish.* Do not "come down off the wall" as Nehemiah was wise to do. "And I sent messengers unto them, saying, I am doing a great work, so that I cannot come down: why should the work cease, whilst I leave it, and come down to you?" (Nehemiah 6:3).

When Oral Roberts began to build the city of Faith...58 floors...his obsession was to combine medicine with the healing of God. He wanted others to know that God uses *physicians and medicine.* He called it *the Gospel for the Whole Man.* God simply wants us well. Life is not just for preparing us for eternity but we can enjoy the here and now. What you eat *matters.* Exercise *matters...in every area...*taking care of your body... *matters.*

But, when Dr. Roberts announced the building of the City of Faith, many doctors rose up against him with anger and tried to destroy his Dream.

Doctors who had taken the oath that they would give themselves to the *healing* and the *health* of people were so angry. They felt it would affect the finances in the other hospitals.

Uncommon Dreams Require Uncommon Determination. Every successful person encounters uncommon opposition. Never forget this. In my book, *The Law of Recognition*, I share 92 facts about understanding the value of an enemy. (You can order this powerful book online at: www.TheWisdomCenter.tv).

5 Reasons Enemies Are Necessary

You Will Always Have An Enemy. Jesus knew this. "And ye shall be hated by all men for My name's sake: but he that endureth to the end the same shall be saved," (Matthew 10:22). Jesus was perfect *and still had an enemy.*

1. Enemies Expose Your Weakness. Enemies birth *humility*...a magnet to others and to God Himself. *Humility is the recognition of what you do not have. It births the ability to value what others do possess.*

2. Enemies Reveal Your Limitations. This forces you to pursue the gifts hidden in those near you. Love is always a map to where the treasure is. *Whatever God Did Not Put In You, He Has Placed In Somebody Near You.*

3. Enemies Are The Bridges Between Obscurity To Significance. David understood this. One day, he was a simple shepherd boy, laughed at and angering his brothers. The next day everyone in Israel was shouting his name...thousands of women were dancing in the streets...*his bills were paid.* Goliath was the *Master Key* that revealed his distinctive difference from others.

4. Your Enemy Will Ultimately Reveal The Greatness Of God To You. Your heart may *doubt.* Your mind may be *confused.* Nevertheless, in a crisis, God will expose His power and love towards you.

5. Enemies Often Force You To Use The Hidden Gifts Stored Within You. Those gifts remain untapped in a climate of comfort.

An Enemy Must Be Conquered, Not Understood. Do not try to understand your adversary. Stay focused.

Who Is An Enemy?

▶ *Your Enemy Is Anyone Who Weakens Your Passion For Your Future And Your Dream.*

▶ *Your Enemy Is Anyone Who Resents Your Progress Or The Goals You Are Pursuing. It Is The People You Trust Who Destroy You.*

▶ *An Enemy Is Anyone Who Had Rather Discuss Your Flaws Than Your Future.*

4 Keys To Overcoming An Enemy

1. Develop Caution And Attention To The Accuracy And Details Of Your Life. Do not give them a reason to attack you.

2. Become Obsessed With Integrity And Accuracy. Guard your goals and your life... carefully. Speak the truth.

3. Consult Mentors Who Have Conquered The Same Opposition. Never attempt to survive a battle without mentorship. Mentors see what you do not see. They know your enemy better than you do. Permit them to speak into your life.

4. Stay Focused On Your Goals At All Times. The Only Weapon Your Enemy Has Is... Distraction. The goal of your adversary is not simply your destruction...or they would have already destroyed you. Their goal is to distract you from your *Assignment*...the problem God created you to solve.

7 Facts About Your Enemies

1. Your Enemy Is Any Person Who Resents Your Desire For Increase And The Rewards It Brings. *Accusations are hurled and often believed causing discomfort and distrust.*

2. You Will Always Have An Enemy. Jesus knew it. "And ye shall be hated of all men for My name's sake: but he that endureth to the end shall be saved," (Matthew 10:22).

3. Your Enemy Is Anyone Who Increases Or Strengthens A Personal Weakness God Is Attempting To Remove From Your Life. *Delilah breathed life into the weakness of Samson. She was his enemy.* (See Judges 16.)

4. Your Enemy Is Anyone That Attempts To Kill The Faith That God Is Birthing Within You. *God may be birthing your ministry. Your enemy is any person who attempts to abort the emergence of that Dream.*

5. Your Enemy Is Anyone Who Would Rather Discuss Your Past Than Your Future. *Yesterday is over. With the masterful stroke of the Master artist, Jesus looked at the woman caught in* *adultery. With a single stroke of mercy, He removed her past and said, "Go and sin no more."* "She said, No man, Lord. And Jesus said unto her, Neither do I condemn thee: go, and sin no more," (John 8:11).

6. Your Enemies Are Sometimes Those Of Your Own Household. *The Holy Spirit will provide answers concerning your enemy. God may lead you into a personal fasting. Fasting will move the hand of God in destroying your enemy.*

7. Your Enemy Will Not Be Allowed By God To Win. *You cannot defeat your enemy in your own strength.* "The Lord is on my side; I will not fear: what can man do unto me?" (Psalm 118:6). "Not that we are sufficient of ourselves to think any thing as of ourselves; but our sufficiency is of God," (2 Corinthians 3:5).

5 Ways The Holy Spirit Will Protect You

1. **The Holy Spirit** *Will Impart Wisdom For Conquering Your Enemy In Your Secret Place Of Prayer.*

2. **The Holy Spirit** *Will Reveal Any Snare Prepared By The Enemy.*

3. **The Holy Spirit** *Within You Is More Powerful Than Any Enemy That You Will Ever Face.*

4. **The Holy Spirit** *Will Demoralize And Weaken Your Enemy With Fear Towards You Before The Battle Even Begins.*

5. **The Holy Spirit** *Will Often Bring Conviction On Your Enemies.*

The Uncommon Dream Will Unleash An Uncommon Enemy.

The Uncommon Dream Is
The Invisible Picture
Of Tomorrow Within You.

-*MIKE MURDOCK*

❦ 8 ❦

THE UNCOMMON DREAM IS THE FORCE THAT CREATES UNCOMMON PEOPLE

Is There Volcanic Energy Within You?

Is it a Volcano of energy...alive and on fire—your Dream?

Millions hate the cycle of their present life. They wake up to a world of mediocrity and sameness. Every morning, they reluctantly step on the *Treadmill of Normality* and start *The Journey to Nowhere.*

God has a better plan. *God has assigned you to do something...NOBODY has ever done before.* Something no one in your family has ever done before.

What Is An Uncommon Dream?

The Uncommon Dream is something you have always wanted to *Experience, Own or Produce.*

It does not matter whatsoever whether others ever accomplish it or not. Everybody around you may appear passive and disinterested.

What matters is that you move in the direction of The Uncommon Dream.

You are closer than you have ever been to launching the greatest season of your entire lifetime.

The Uncommon Dream Is The Invisible

Picture Of Tomorrow Within You. Desire is the miracle. Feed it and it will become a strong desire. Fuel it more and it will become an *obsession*.

Uncommon People Think Uncommon Thoughts. When it is possible, it would be worth your time to listen to the Martin Luther King documentary of the Dream he had. It is hard to believe there was a time when women were not permitted to vote. It was as if they were less than human...that the color of your skin would determine what you could and could not do.

Martin Luther King had a message: *"I have a Dream."* I think it is worth listening to *repeatedly*. He stirred up The Seeds of Greatness among his people that it was possible to have a place in life where you can be treated with honor...respected as a normal human being.

His Dream cost him his life.

Your Obsession Will Unlock Your Greatness. Your obsession for your Dream must be an irresistible magnet that pulls others toward you to participate. *Your Obsession Will Birth Passion.*

Passion is a current that decides what comes to you or moves away from you. Your Dream is the rival to your Distractions and Adversaries. Your joy does not matter to many of them.

- ▶ Your Future...*Is Just Ahead.*
- ▶ Your Happiest Days...*Are Just Ahead.*
- ▶ Everything You Have Ever Wanted...*Is About To Come To Pass.*

Every moment you give to your Dream will energize, strengthen you, and bring you great joy.

The Uncommon Dream is within you.
Nobody can see it...but you.

8 Rewards Of Keeping Focused On Your Dream

1. **The Uncommon Dream** *Will Intimidate Those Who Are Fearful Because They Have Not Determined Their Own Dreams.*

2. **The Uncommon Dream** *Will Arouse Unhappy Voices Around You.* God will then use them as Golden Keys to Unlocking The Treasury of Uncommon Ideas for you.

3. **The Uncommon Dream** *Will Eliminate Wrong People From Your Life.*

4. **The Uncommon Dream** *Is A Seed For Birthing Tomorrow.*

5. **The Uncommon Dream** *Drives You Away From Your Present...Gives Birth To Your Future.*

6. **The Uncommon Dream** *Is Your Invisible Companion On Every Journey Through Life... Accompanying You Every Step Of The Way.*

7. **The Uncommon Dream** *Is Like A Hidden Seed.* It is there even when you do not feel it... responsive to the refreshing water of right words and environment.

8. **The Uncommon Dream** *Unlocks Invisible Seeds Of Passion Presently Dormant In Your Mind.*

Take time to consider what you need to tell others about your Dream. Disappointments, conflicts and *unexpected obstacles* may block your vision.

When you stop visualizing The Uncommon Dream...depression will suffocate you. That is why you need to know how to stay motivated toward your Dream.

The Uncommon Dream Is The Force That Creates Uncommon People.

RECOMMENDED FOR YOUR WISDOM LIBRARY:
B-11   Dream Seeds (106 pages/$9)
B-13   Seeds of Wisdom on Dreams & Goals, Vol. 1 (32
        pages/$3)
B-74   The Assignment: The Dream & The Destiny, Vol. 1
        (164 pages/$10)
TS-11   Dream Seeds (6 tapes/$30)
TS-19   The Double Diamond Principle In Dreams, Decisions
        & Destiny (6 tapes/$30)

❧ 9 ❧

THE UNCOMMON DREAM WILL BRING REWARDS TO YOUR ENTIRE FAMILY

Nobody Else Can Be Like You.
Whatever Is Inside You Will Change Everyone Around You. *God planned you. You are unlike anyone else on earth.*

Here is the account of Joseph in the book of Genesis. The life of Joseph excites Uncommon Achievers. Joseph's Dreams brought rewards to his family. "And Joseph dreamed a dream, and he told it his brethren: and they hated him yet the more. And he said unto them, Hear, I pray you, this dream which I have dreamed: For, behold, we were binding sheaves in the field, and, lo, my sheaf arose, and also stood upright; and, behold, your sheaves stood round about, and made obeisance to my sheaf. And his brethren said to him, Shalt thou indeed reign over us? or shalt thou indeed have dominion over us? And they hated him yet the more for his dreams, and for his words. And he dreamed yet another dream, and told it his brethren, and said, Behold, I have dreamed a dream more; and, behold, the sun and the moon and the eleven stars made obeisance to me. And he told it to his father, and to his brethren: and his father rebuked him, and said unto him, What is this dream that thou hast dreamed? Shall I and thy mother and thy brethren indeed come to bow down ourselves to thee to the earth? And his brethren envied him; but his father observed the saying," (Genesis 37:5-11).

Famine would have destroyed the Egyptians but Joseph was *their reward. He had the ability to interpret dreams*, which proved to be a message from God to Pharaoh.

Remember Wisdom Key #54: *Your Significance Is Not In Your Similarity To Another, But In Your Point Of Difference From Another.* Grasp this.

God is not a duplicator. He is a creator. You are perfect and genetically accurate for solving a specific problem for somebody on earth.

It is important that you realize you are not needed everywhere. You are needed at a *specific place, time and for a specific person.* Do not take offense at this. It is all in God's plan.

Joseph's brothers hated the attention his father showed him. They despised his *distinction*.

Joseph says, "Here I pray you this dream which I have dreamed," and he explains the Dream to them. *Nothing is more shocking than to trust those who do not trust you.*

Why did Joseph tell his brothers?

Because when God puts something in your heart...you want to share it. When God puts a Dream inside you...a goal...a picture of something you can do or have...you want to involve others.

Your Dream is different from your Assignment.

Your *Assignment* is the problem you solve.

Your *Dream* is the reward you receive for doing

your Assignment. God did not give Joseph a picture of his responsibilities. He gave him a picture of his rewards.

An Uncommon Dream From God Will Create Separation. Those closest to you may not understand. Opposition will often come from those closest to you. Joseph's brothers sold him into slavery but God protected him. God had a plan to fulfill in his life. "The Lord was with Joseph, and he was a prosperous man," (Genesis 39:2). Joseph found grace in His eyes. The Lord blessed the Egyptians.

Potiphar's wife was attracted to Joseph. She wanted him. She pursued him *desperately,* but he continually refused. Yet, she falsely accused him for something he did not do. Everyone *believed* her. *Yes, this could happen to you, too.* Many ministers have even experienced a crucifixion of their credibility in the media.

When Your Uncommon Dream Dies

▶ *What do you do when your Dream dies?*
▶ *What do you do when you are falsely accused and everyone believes the lies?*
▶ *What do you do when your reputation has been stained?*
▶ *What do you do when your credibility has been destroyed?*
▶ *What do you do when you cannot protect yourself?*

Joseph Became A Problem-Solver In A Prison He Did Not Deserve. Joseph kept a sweet spirit. He did not discuss the false accusations. *Meditation, Mind,*

Conversations…give life.
Stop discussing what you want to die.

Paint Your Mind With The Uncommon Dream

Elijah "painted the picture" of a Dream for the widow of Zarephath (see 1 Kings 17).

She could not Dream anymore. Her Dream had died when she saw her sickened son dying. This was their last meal. God had turned off the brook's supply.

God brought Elijah to the widow's house to breathe new life into her Dream. It was the Dream that provoked her to *obedience.*

The greatness of Elijah did not impress the widow. Neither did his *charisma,* his *anointed* words…nor his *aura* impress her.

She simply heard a man of God saying…her provision cruise of oil would not fail. She would not have to worry about her future. *God would supply.*

Elijah painted an Uncommon Dream on her mind. *She decided to believe it.*

What was her mind picture before his arrival? *Death.* He saw it on her face. He heard it in her words. She had no faith. There was *nobody else* to talk life into her. Nobody in her life saw her future. She did not have a future…until a prophet spoke.

Words Are The Seeds For Feelings.
Words Are The Seeds For Persuasion.

What the widow saw around her was so visible…so dominating. The only thing she could see was her present.

Then, a man of God stepped into her life and said,

"Let me tell you what your future can be."

Something In Your Hand Is Your Seed That Will Create Any Future You Want (see Luke 6:38).

She *listened.* Her heart believed...she said, "If a Seed is the price of my future I will sow it." She reaped the rewards of *obedience*...the reward of her Uncommon Dream. "And she went and did according to the saying of Elijah: and she, and he, and her house, did eat many days," (2 Kings 17:15).

Remember Wisdom Key #4: *When You Let Go Of What Is In Your Hand, God Will Let Go Of What Is In His Hand.*

RECOMMENDED FOR YOUR WISDOM LIBRARY:
B-122   Seeds of Wisdom on Your Assignment, Vol. 20
      (32 pages/$5)
B-126   Seeds of Wisdom on Mentorship, Vol. 24 (32 pages/$5)
B-143   My Personal Dream Book (32 pages/$5)
TS-02   The Grasshopper Complex (6 tapes/$30)

An Uncommon Dream
Will Require
An Uncommon Mentor.

-*MIKE MURDOCK*

~ **10** ~

THE UNCOMMON DREAM WILL REQUIRE AN UNCOMMON MENTOR

You Cannot Succeed Alone.

Nobody ever has. Nobody ever will. You see, two are always better than one. Two are better than one...and a threefold cord is not easily broken. "And if one prevail against him, two shall withstand him; and a threefold cord is not quickly broken," (Ecclesiastes 4:12).

Mentorship is the transference of Wisdom.

Wisdom is not genetic. You can be a stupid father like Saul, and have a brilliant son like Jonathan. *Wisdom* is the difference between your prosperity and poverty. *Wisdom* is the difference between seasons.

What Is Mentorship?

► Mentorship Is Wisdom Without The Wait.
► Mentorship Is Success Without The Pain.
► Mentorship Is Learning Through The Losses Of Another.

What Is A Mentor?

► The Uncommon Mentor is a trusted teacher.

► The Uncommon Mentor focuses on your future. Few truly discern an Uncommon Mentor God has brought into their life. That explains why success takes so long to obtain...for so many.

Your Goals Choose Your Mentor. Elisha wanted a double portion of the anointing that flowed through the prophet Elijah. Those *goals... desire...passion* birthed his reaching for Elijah.

► The Master Secret To Life Is Wisdom.
► The Master Secret To Wisdom Is... Asking.
► Your Questions Reveal Your Passion.

The Queen of Sheba pursued and asked questions of Solomon. She trusted him for the correct answers. *What questions are you asking?*

2 Ways To Receive Wisdom

Mistakes And Mentors.

Experience is God's *slowest* way of teaching. God uses *mistakes* to teach fools who are unwilling to sit at the feet of a Mentor.

The Uncommon Mentor is a Master Key to achieving The Uncommon Dream.

Here are some powerful facts about your relationship with your Mentors.

9 Facts About The Uncommon Mentor

1. **The Uncommon Mentor Is Your Coach, Not Your Cheerleader.**
2. **The Uncommon Mentor May Not Tell You What You Are Doing Right; But, What You**

Are Doing Wrong.

3. The Uncommon Mentor Will Not Compliment You. He Will Correct You.

4. The Uncommon Mentor Will Not Justify Your Failure. He Will Expose The Reason For It.

5. The Uncommon Mentor Does Not Ignore Your Flaws. He Helps You Overcome Them.

6. The Uncommon Mentor Is An Experienced Adviser. He Sees Something You Do Not See.

7. The Uncommon Mentor Will Know Something You Do Not Know.

8. The Uncommon Mentor Will See Possible Pitfalls And Potential Traps That You Cannot See.

9. It Is Your Responsibility To Pursue And Develop A Strong Relationship With An Uncommon Mentor. Elisha pursued Elijah. Ruth pursued Naomi.

When you discover your Dream, it is only then you will recognize the Mentor...worthy of pursuit.

Famous, exceptional champions in the world today had or continue to have someone close to their life who speaks strong counsel *continually* into them.

These Mentors want them to succeed and make progress toward their Dreams. Their *compassion, caring and expertise* is worth a small fortune to you if you will take the time to *listen, inquire,* and be *appreciative*.

Mentors Impart Credibility

One of my favorite illustrations is about the old lawyer who had lunch with the young lawyer just graduated from college.

Going back to his office after lunch, the old, legendary and famous lawyer draped his arm on the shoulder of the youthful one.

They walked slowly back to their offices. Many people saw them.

When the young lawyer walked back in his own office, he was so discouraged. He had hoped for some recommendations from the lawyer on specific cases. He had wanted the old lawyer to give him some of his business.

The young lawyer was almost destitute financially. He knew it takes time to get your own clients and build integrity in the eyes of a community.

"He could have given me several cases that would have made all the difference in the world for me," he cried dejectedly to himself.

However, the next week several phone calls came. In the coming weeks, numerous cases came his way. What had happened?

Those who had observed that the legendary lawyer was conferring and associating with the young lawyer started believing in the potential and future of the young lawyer. I call it the *"transference of credibility."*

You will need people who can share their experiences with you. Some have tasted failure, and others can share the specific reasons why they did not fail.

Make a connection with someone whose influence you admire! You need those who will correct you and make you think twice about an important decision.

Encouragers are vital. You will need and benefit

from honest confrontation. One of my biggest regrets is failure to have qualified honest people who would confront me about decisions and directions I was taking over the years.

Favor Is When Others Want To Help You. They believe in you. Sometimes, they do not even understand why this mysterious desire to aid you even exists. However, their Wisdom can make your life a thousand times easier.

Reach for intercessors.

Reach for Mentors. Especially those who are *Godly*, *mature* and *compassionate...seasoned.* "Again I say unto you, That if two of you shall agree on earth as touching any thing that they shall ask, it shall be done for them of My Father which is in heaven," (Matthew 18:19).

A young man who was traveling with me was telling everybody he was my protegé.

I stopped him and said, "Tell me the last three questions you have asked me." *He could not name one.*

I said, "You have made serious choices that affect the rest of your life without even consulting me. In fact, you have done it secretly. I do not want anyone to think I am accountable for the kinds of decisions you have made. That is an embarrassment to me." Remember Wisdom Key #297: *The Pursuit Of The Mentor Reveals The Passion Of The Protegé.*

Your Choice Of Mentors Reveals Much

▶ When I know who is Mentoring You...*I will know your priorities.*

▶ When I see Naomi, *I know what Ruth*

contains.

▶ When I listen to Paul, *I have the information Timothy used for decision-making.*

▶ When I look at Mordecai, *I can discern the principles inside of Esther.*

▶ When I study the life of Moses, *I understand the turning points of Joshua.*

Your Mentor May Not Be Your Best Friend

▶ **Your Best Friend** loves you the way you are.
Your Mentor loves you too much to leave you the way you are.

▶ **Your Best Friend** is comfortable with your past.
Your Mentor is comfortable with your future.

▶ **Your Best Friend** will risk your success to keep your approval.
Your Mentor will risk your affection to help you succeed.

8 Hindrances To Recognizing The Uncommon Mentor

1. **Pride Can Blind You To The Uncommon Mentor.** The Pharisees were filled with pride and did not recognize Jesus the Son of God.

2. **Guilt Can Blind You To The Uncommon Mentor.** When people feel guilty over a sin in their lives...the presence of a holy man will intimidate them.

3. Jealousy Often Blinds You To The Uncommon Mentor. Jealousy and envy have robbed us of many blessings God has in store for us.

4. Wrong Voices Of Influence Can Blind You To The Uncommon Mentor. It is dangerous when parents speak disrespectfully about a man of God in the presence of their children.

5. Prejudiced Mentors Can Blind You To The Uncommon Mentor. Be careful to not *unconsciously* perpetuate prejudices of others.

6. Arrogance Can Blind You To The Uncommon Mentor. The arrogance of Haman blinded him to the greatness of Mordecai.

7. Your Personal Agenda Can Blind You To The Uncommon Mentor. It is important to recognize a man of God even when you fail to hear the Voice of God *personally*.

8. Familiarity Often Blinds You To The Uncommon Mentor. Pastors experience this often. Because their congregations see them often...their humanity is evident and too often people focus on *weaknesses*. Family members suffer greatly because of *familiarity*.

Regardless, whether it is a pastor, adviser, Mentor...*You Will Need To Be In Submission To Someone During The Process Of Your Uncommon Dream.*

Every Friendship Nurtures
A Strength Or A Weakness.

-MIKE MURDOCK

≈ 11 ≈
THE UNCOMMON DREAM WILL BIRTH CHANGES IN YOUR RELATIONSHIPS

Your Dream Decides Who Enjoys You.

The Uncommon Dream decides who belongs with you. Nurture relationships connected to your Dream.

You need motivators and people to encourage you. Who are the top ten people necessary to complete and birth The Dream in your heart? You will need people who are *genuine, sincere* and *caring* toward you.

Golden Connections Are Vital Instruments And Bridges...sent into your life to help you make it at the curve of change. There will be times of disillusionment. You may become disappointed with yourself.

You will need someone *who will talk faith words and victory words into your mind.*

You will need someone *who is not distracted by your burdens or unassociated with your fears and pain.*

You will need someone *who treasures your difference from themselves.*

You Will Need Uncommon Friendships To Achieve An Uncommon Dream. Remember

Wisdom Key #326: *Those Who Cannot Increase You Will Inevitably Decrease You.*

Friendships Feed Your Fear Or Faith. Identify those who...*create your comfort...and build your faith.*

Question Checklist

▶ Who Are Your Friends?
▶ Do You Admire Them?
▶ Do They Admire You?
▶ Who Do You Permit Close To Your Life?
▶ Do They Build Your Faith Or Increase Your Fears?
▶ Who Has Discerned Your Greatness?
▶ Who Recognizes Your Uncommon Traits?

Discern Who Responds Most To You

If you are going to accomplish your Dream, it will take the assistance of others to do it.

Make reference to your Dream in telephone conversations when appropriate. When your friends request a gift list from you, give them a gift idea linked to the completion of your Dream.

Your own passion for your Dream will increase as you communicate the importance of your Dream to others. Your family and friends will become familiar with your future and want to help you obtain your Dream.

Few friends will remain in your life forever. Friendships are usually seasonal...depending on your pursuit and convenience. *Do not waste your energy on friendships that do not energize your life.*

Those who admire your Dream will want to participate and become involved. When you want to go fishing, those who love fishing will come. When you want to see a movie, those who love movies will want to go with you.

Relationships will always change relative to your focus and passion.

My dear friend, Sherman Owens, taught me to, "Listen to unhappy people for ideas." This is so important. Everybody hurts somewhere. Some hide it. Some express it.

However, when you begin to listen to the pain around you, ideas will emerge for solving that pain. *Those solutions bring rewards. Your solution will create a friendship.*

Your Dream Must Be Personal. It is essential that you discover your Dream and give yourself totally to it. "Let every man abide in the same calling wherein he was called," (1 Corinthians 7:20).

It is a useless waste of time to pursue what others have in mind for your life. God has a plan.

God is not a respecter of persons. He created *you* for a special time and season.

He created *you* for a specific purpose. However, *your own choices* will determine your destiny.

The Holy Spirit Is Faithful To Assist You In Your Dream. "For thou shalt go to all that I shall send thee, and whatsoever I command thee thou shalt speak. Be not afraid of their faces: for I am with thee to deliver thee, saith the Lord," (Jeremiah 1:7-8).

> ▶ *Your Dream* will struggle to live...like a rose in a garden of weeds.

> ▶ *Your Dream* will sometimes struggle to

receive sunshine...in a world of darkness.

▶ ***Your Dream*** *will thirst for water among the thorns of frustration.*

When your battle is the most difficult, that is usually an indication that you are at the very scene of the fulfillment of your Dream.

Never discuss your Dream carelessly with unconcerned friends.

Remember Wisdom Key #123: *Every Friendship Nurtures A Strength Or A Weakness.*

Your Uncommon Dream Will Birth Changes In Your Relationships.

RECOMMENDED FOR YOUR WISDOM LIBRARY:

B-14   Seeds of Wisdom on Relationships, Vol. 2
          (32 pages/$3)
B-58   The Mentor's Manna on Attitude (32 pages/$3)
B-97   The Assignment: The Trials & The Triumphs, Vol. 3
          (160 pages/$10)
TS-16 The Double Diamond Principle In Successful
          Relationships (6 tapes/$30)

❦ 12 ❦

THE UNCOMMON DREAM WILL REQUIRE THE MIRACLE HAND OF GOD

God Designs The Future...You Choose It.
It is your responsibility to discern the Dream. *God will never birth a Dream within you that is achievable without Him.*

You cannot succeed without God. Jesus made it clear. *Ask...Seek...Knock...*go behind closed doors. You have no right to anything you have not pursued. Honor the capabilities of another. Remember Wisdom Key #98: *Any Step Toward Self-Sufficiency Is A Step Away From God.*

▶ Asking Is The *Proof Of Honor.*
▶ Asking Is The *Proof Of Humility.*
▶ Asking Is The *Proof Of Respect.*

What is your *Dream...*your *Goal?* If it matters to you...it matters to God. Who have you chosen to believe? What do you want your future to be like? What???

When You Decide What You Want, God Will Get Involved. He gives you The Uncommon Dream to keep you connected to Him and perpetuate His plans and desires. It requires God and His Wisdom to complete that Dream.

2 Keys To Expecting Miracles

1. Decide The Miracle You Want. Faith Requires A Focus. When you give faith an option, it shuts down. It quits. Faith requires clarity. Do you know what you really want? What is your real Dream? What do you want God to do?

2. When You Decide What You Want, God Will Get Involved. Ten inches away from Jesus Christ, there was a woman who had hemorrhaged for 12 years. She did not receive her healing at that time. One inch away from Him, reaching...she did not receive her healing. *She had to touch Him.*

The blind man received no attention from Jesus. Jesus was walking by. When the blind man cried out, he showed uncommon passion...he knew what he really wanted...*Jesus got involved.*

God Never Responds To Your Pain, He Only Responds To Your Pursuit.

The Uncommon Dream will always require the assistance of others. *Golden Connections are necessary.* Joseph could have never reached the palace...without the butler connecting him to Pharaoh. Jesus rarely gave "altar calls" to Pharisees. He went home with Zacchaeus, the tax collector. *Why?* He responds to passion in others.

Your Dream Is Personalized...By God.

▶ Your Dream Is Connected To Your *Personality*.

▶ Your Dream Is Connected To Your *Imagination*.

▶ Your Dream Is Connected To Your *Gifts*.

I am not talking about when you eat too much pizza or spaghetti late at night. I am not talking about that type of Dream.

I am talking about a *Goal*...an *Obsession*... *Something* you want to *have, do or become.*

It is always on your mind. It is inside you and is growing or dying. It is *increasing or decreasing.*

Nobody sees it but you.

As you discern your *gifts, talents* and *abilities* involved for your Dream...Remember the following:

3 Important Keys

1. *God Has Qualified You To Be A Perfect Solution For Somebody.*
2. *It Is The Responsibility Of Others To Discern Your Assignment To Them.*
3. *When You Discover To Whom You Have Been Assigned, You Will Experience Great Peace, Fulfillment And Provision For Your Life.*

I once asked a young man what he intended to become.

He replied, "A doctor."

"Has that always been a lifetime Dream from childhood?" I asked.

"Not really. My mother has always felt like that would be something good for me to do. So, I guess I will try that," was his *uncertain* reply.

How sad! He will not do well. In fact, he will probably drop out of Medical School before his time of completion. *Why?* You will only persist in something that offers a powerful *pleasure, benefit, or advantage.*

Your Uncommon Dream Must Be Strong Enough To Keep Your Interest And Attention. *The Uncommon Dream will qualify those who deserve access to you.* Move toward your goal...your *Dream.*

Make any investment necessary.

Sometimes it may require a change in location.

Be willing to *pay the price.*

Create, *develop* and *make* your Uncommon Dream become a reality. Remember Wisdom Key #343: *Champions Make Decisions That Create The Future They Desire; Losers Make Decisions That Create The Present They Desire.*

The Uncommon Dream Will Require The Miracle Hand Of God.

❧ 13 ❧

THE UNCOMMON DREAM MUST BECOME YOUR TOTAL OBSESSION

━━━━━➤〇◄━━━━━

The Obsession Of Jesus Was To Finish.
He wanted to reach the conclusion of His Assignment on earth. He thought it...He talked it...He lived it. "Jesus saith unto them, My meat is to do the will of Him that sent Me, and *to finish* His work," (John 4:34).

Jesus considered Non-Finishers disqualified for the kingdom. "Jesus saith unto him, No man, having put his hand to the plough, and looking back, is fit for the kingdom of God," (Luke 9:62).

You will never leave where you are now until you know exactly where you want to be. Remember Wisdom Key #129: *If You Do Not Know Where You Belong, You Will Adapt To Where You Are.*

You must know exactly what you want before you can obtain it. You will never change your *location* until you determine your *destination.*

When you are consumed and passionate about your Dream, you will discover an atmosphere of victory and confidence surrounds you.

Jackie Holland is a dear friend in Dallas, Texas, who longed for years to feed the hungry.

Finally, she decided one day to take the food she

had from her own kitchen, drive to the neglected and homeless areas of Dallas, and feed the people out of the trunk of her car. After doing this for some time, she decided to involve others.

Her testimony is miraculous.

Today, she oversees a remarkable ministry to the poor, and executives have given her thousands of dollars for food. Across the world, people are talking about her. She has also been on major television shows.

Life always opens the doors widest to the passionate people with purpose.

Your Dream Must Become An Obsession.

You will create an atmosphere and climate around you that others cannot resist.

There are so many people without a purpose and need a passion in their lives. They will feel your energy...join you and assist you in your goals.

Those who have a passion themselves will respect it. Those who are uncertain about their Assignment will gratefully identify and connect with you to help you achieve your Dream.

Those close to you will fuel your fire. *They will recognize your passion. They will celebrate your focus.*

5 Keys To Developing An Obsession For Your Dream

1. **Refuse Any Weight Or Distraction To Your Dream.** "Let us lay aside every weight, and the sin that doth so easily beset us, and let us run with patience the race that is set before us," (Hebrews 12:1).

2. **Be Ruthless In Severing Any Ties To A**

Project Not Connected To Your Dream. He instructed Timothy, "No man that warreth entangleth himself with the affairs of this life; that he may please Him who hath chosen him to be a soldier," (2 Timothy 2:4).

3. Constantly Study Your Dream. He urged Timothy, "Study to shew thyself approved unto God, a workman that needeth not to be ashamed, rightly dividing the word of truth," (2 Timothy 2:15).

4. Shun Conversations That Are Unrelated To Your Dream. "But shun profane and vain babblings: for they will increase unto more ungodliness. But foolish and unlearned questions avoid, knowing that they do gender strife," (2 Timothy 2:16, 23).

5. Learn To Disconnect From Any Relationship That Does Not Feed Your Addiction To His Presence And Your Obsession To Complete The Dream God Has Given To You. "And if any man obey not our word by this epistle, note that man, and have no company with him, that he may be ashamed," (2 Thessalonians 3:14).

Take Time To Ask Yourself These Questions And Answer Them Honestly:

1. *What is your specific lifetime Dream?*
2. *What goals have you set that energize you?*
3. *What do you consider is a worthy Dream?*
4. *What is the most important thing you want others to remember about you?*
5. *Are you pursuing a Dream that requires the constant encouragement of others?*
6. *Do you have to persuade others to follow you toward your Dream?*

7.   *Are your decisions causing you to fail?*

8.   *Have you decided not to achieve something spectacular with your life?*

Your Dream Must Have Your Focus.

Have you ever seen the little child play with his food? He is not *hungry*. He is *playful*. He wants to get out of the chair and run with his friends.

Many people live life like that. They never really abandon themselves to what is, *"the magnificent obsession."* Your Dream must be big enough to attract your attention.

You Already Have Everything You Need To Give Birth To The Uncommon Dream

▶ Your Dream Must Originate In The Heart Of God Before Its Fulfillment Will Satisfy You.

▶ You Must Be Persuaded It Is From The Heart Of God.

▶ You Must Be Willing To Fight For And Protect Your Dream From Criticism And Any Satanic Substitutions.

▶ You Must Discern Any Distractions To Your Dream Immediately And Refuse Its Having Any Place In Your Life.

▶ Your Dream Must Have Time And Attention To Germinate And Come Into Clear Focus.

▶ Your Dream Must Become The Dominate Obsession Of Your Life Filling Up Every Available Space Within You, Crowding

Out Every Distraction And Every
Adversary.

▶ *The Proof Of Your Passion Is The Investment Of Time.* Whatever has the ability to keep your attention has mastered you.

▶ *You Will Only Succeed When You Develop An Obsession For Your Dream.*

What You Respect
You Will Attract.

-MIKE MURDOCK

≈ **14** ≈

THE UNCOMMON DREAM WILL REQUIRE YOUR PERSONAL RESPECT

What You Respect You Will Attract.

You Must Respect What You Want To Come Toward You. Jesus taught that those who respected and appreciated what they had would receive even more. "Well done, thou good and faithful servant: thou hast been faithful over a few things, I will make thee ruler over many things: enter thou into the joy of thy lord," (Matthew 25:21).

The Uncommon Dream is like an invisible magnet...a desired miracle or blessing you want from God. It must be something worthy of your respect and worthy of pursuit.

You must despise where you are before you will ever be where you desire to be.

When you boldly announce your Uncommon Dream, you instantly create a Golden Connection and bond with every other person who wanted to accomplish such a Dream as well.

Decisiveness Changes The Atmosphere. It energizes every person around you.

Make every hour produce a specific task for you.

Your Dream Deserves Your Time

▶ Identify Time-Wasters.

▶ Stop Doing Tasks That Do Not Affect The Outcome Of Your Dreams.

▶ Define Your Expectations Of Those Around You.

▶ Explain To Others Their Part In Fulfilling Your Dream.

▶ Write Shorter Letters.

▶ Keep Your Phone Calls To Two Minutes.

The Uncommon Dream deserves your immediate and total attention. Do not wait for great things.

Move now. Move quickly and decisively.

The Uncommon Dream Will Birth Uncommon Habits

To succeed in your planning and identifying time-wasters...you must birth good habits. Establish habits that show respect whether it is for your body, relationships, or finances.

Remember Wisdom Key #353: *Those Who Do Not Respect Your Time Will Not Respect Your Wisdom Either.*

Habits Decide Your Future.

One of the wealthiest women in Dallas, Texas focused on developing one of the greatest companies for women.

Every morning, beginning in 1963, she wrote down her plans for the day. For more than 38 years, she selected six things to accomplish and prioritize.

When she passed away, her company was worth more than $1.2 billion dollars. Her personal worth was over $300 million dollars. *She focused on her Dream, and birthed a habit of planning every day.*

The Morning Habits Of Mohammed Ali.

One of my favorite people is Mohammed Ali. He and I were staying at the same hotel in my hometown in Lake Charles, Louisiana. I had the privilege of talking with him.

When he was Cassias Clay, 18 years old, he saw a picture of himself as a heavyweight champion of the world. He was already boxing...and he began to get up early for special roadwork...4:30 a.m.

Champions Willingly Do Daily What Ordinary Men Do Occasionally.

3 Habits That Can Change Your Life

1. Write Down Your Daily Plan Every Morning. It does not have to be lengthy in detail. A simple sheet of paper with a list of seven things you want to accomplish...that very day.

2. Enter The Secret Place For Prayer... At The Same Time Each Morning. Remember Wisdom Key #274: *Where You Are Determines What You Hear; What You Hear Determines What You Believe.*

Birds require air. Fish require water. *Uncommon men and women of God require the presence of God. Pursue His presence.* Get alone with Him.

The Secret Place is the only place you will receive Uncommon Wisdom *without the stain of human logic and limitations.*

3. Read The Word Of God Each Morning...Without Fail. His Word is His Wisdom. The wisest man who ever lived decreed, "Wisdom is the principal thing," (Proverbs 4:7). "Keep therefore and do them; for this is your wisdom and your understanding in the sight of the nations, which shall hear all these statutes, and say, Surely this great nation is a wise and understanding people," (Deuteronomy 4:6).

Who Is Disrespecting Your Dream?

Years ago, I became involved with a great organization. A young man that I signed up in the multi-level marketing plan was ecstatic with joy. He had caught the vision.

He was convinced his efforts would be profitable. It was a proven company. Thousands had already done well. He could hardly wait to get home and tell his family.

A few days later I still had not heard from him... I called him. "I am anxious to see you at the meeting tomorrow night," I said enthusiastically. "Uh, I do not think I will be able to come." He sounded quite discouraged. I responded with, "Of course, you will!" "No, I talked to my family about my dreams and goals and they simply laughed."

What had happened? The young man's family did not see the *picture* he was looking at. They did not have the information he possessed. They were *undecided, unlearned and unfocused.*

His very enthusiasm *intimidated* them.

Millions of people are discontented with life. Their hearts have never caught fire. Their mind is like a huge field without any Seed sown into it. They will not produce *greatness, pursue,* nor *respect* it.

Develop respect for yourself...your Dream.

Your future depends on it. Dare to Dream bigger dreams than you have ever dreamed before.

When you allow God to rule and direct your Dreams, you can experience unlimited miracles. *Uncommon Dreams...are worthy of pursuit.*

The Uncommon Dream Will Require Your Personal Respect.

An Uncommon Dream
Requires
Uncommon Faith.

-MIKE MURDOCK

✎ 15 ✎

THE UNCOMMON DREAM WILL REQUIRE UNCOMMON FAITH

Faith Attracts The Attention Of God.

To achieve The Uncommon Dream you must learn to use the most explosive weapon God has given you: Your Faith.

You do not have to drive a Rolls Royce to impress Him. Nor is it necessary to be a Harvard graduate.

23 Facts Every Dreamer Should Know About Faith

1. *God Is Impressed When You Use The Faith He Has Already Given You.* "...God hath dealt to every man the measure of faith," (Romans 12:3).

2. *Faith Is That Invisible Confidence That Something Exists Other Than What You Presently See.*

3. *Faith Is That Internal Belief System Planted In You By God.*

4. *Faith Is The Ability To Believe.*

5. *Faith Stimulates Incredible Favor From God And His Angels.*

6. *Faith Is The Magnet That Attracts God Toward You.*

7. *Faith Is What Drives Ordinary Men To*

Accomplish The Extraordinary.

    8. *Faith Is The Magic Ingredient To Every Miracle.*

    9. *Faith Is What Turns Common People Into Uncommon Achievers.*

    10. *Faith Can Transform You From A Weakling Into The Champion God Intended You To Be.*

    11. *Faith Is A Seed Planted Into The Soil Of Your Spirit.* God planted it there at your birth.

    12. *Faith Is Invisible To The Natural Eye, Like Minerals In The Water.* Yet, it is very tangible in the realm of The Spirit.

    13. *Faith Is Like A Muscle...The More You Use It The Stronger It Will Become.*

    14. *Your Faith Decides The Miracles, The Blessings And The Dreams You Obtain.*

    15. *The Difference In Personalities And Talents Does Not Limit How We Decide To Use Our Faith.* We *must focus our believing toward our dreams.*

    16. *Your Future Is Decided By Who You Choose To Believe.*

    17. *Your Faith Is An Invisible Substance.* Like the wind or electricity, you may not see it with your natural eye, but its presence and force is proven by its results in your life. "Now faith is the substance of things hoped for, the evidence of things not seen," (Hebrews 11:1).

    18. *You Already Possess The Seed Of Faith Within You.* Whatever you choose to believe decides whether it will be productive or destructive to your life. "God hath dealt to every man the measure of faith," (Romans 12:3).

    19. *Whenever You Use Your Faith, You Please*

The Heart Of God. Faith is very important to God. He wants you to believe every word He says. He is insulted by unbelief.

20. *You Will Change Your Circumstances When You Change The Direction Of Your Believing.* You will inevitably experience what you consistently believe.

21. *Your Biggest Mountain Will Succumb To Your Smallest Seed Of Faith.* You may feel as though your faith is weak. I have felt that way. You must act on your faith. Speak to that mountain and keep on speaking when it seems to refuse to budge. When you learn this secret, the mountains in your life will begin to move.

22. *You Must Pursue What You Really Believe God Wants You To Possess.* Miracles do not just happen where they are needed. Miracles happen where they are wanted.

23. *Your Guarantee Of Eternal Life Hinges Upon Your Faith In Jesus Christ.* "For God so loved the world, that He gave His only begotten Son, that whosoever believeth in Him should not perish, but have everlasting life," (John 3:16).

What Dream Dominates Your Mind?

It may appear unattainable. It may seem impossible, yet the picture persists within you. There is a reason.

You must conquer your doubts. It is an important key to achieving your Dream.

You see, God begins every miracle in your life with a Seed-picture. God plants these pictures as Invisible Seeds within us.

It is important to make sure your Dream is in line with God's Word and is from Him. *Miracles* and *Blessings* are His rewards for our faith in Him.

▶ *What do you Dream of doing with your life?*

▶ *What blessing are you pursuing?*

▶ *What would you attempt to do if you knew it was impossible to fail?*

▶ *What miracle picture has God planted in your heart?*

▶ *What desired Dream dominates your mind?*

Exercise your faith in God. Through Him, all things are possible. "And Jesus looking upon them saith, With men it is impossible, but not with God: for with God all things are possible," (Mark 10:27).

Nothing will increase your faith like The Word of God. Remember Wisdom Key # 329: *Your Faith Decides Your Miracles.*

7 Rewards For Reading The Word Of God

1. The Word Of God Cleanses Your Conscience. "Now ye are clean through the word which I have spoken unto you," (John 15:3).

2. The Word Of God Warns Of Pitfalls. "Thy word have I hid in my heart, that I might not sin against Thee," (Psalm 119:11).

3. The Word Of God Births Uncommon Joy. "These things have I spoken unto you, that My joy might remain in you, and that your joy might be full," (John 15:11).

4. The Word Of God Is The Source Of

Wisdom In Your Life. "For the Lord giveth wisdom: out of His mouth cometh knowledge and understanding," (Proverbs 2:6).

5. The Word Of God Solves Every Battle. "Thou through Thy commandments hast made me wiser than mine enemies," (Psalm 119:98).

6. The Word Of God Corrects You. "Wherewithal shall a young man cleanse his way? by taking heed thereto according to Thy word," (Psalm 119:9).

7. The Word Of God Can Solve Your Mental Problems. "Great peace have they that love Thy law," (Psalm 119:165).

The Uncommon Dream Will Require Uncommon Faith.

Miracles Do Not Go
Where They Are Needed;
They Go Where They
Are Expected.

-MIKE MURDOCK

⇜ 16 ⇝
THE UNCOMMON DREAM REQUIRES SUPERNATURAL INTERVENTION

⟫⦁⟪

Your Dream Will Require Miracles.
Your Father refuses to be forgotten and ignored.
▶ *Miracles Will Require God.*
▶ *God Requires Obedience.*

When *Joshua and the Israelites* approached Jericho, it took a *miracle* for the walls to come down.

When *Gideon and his 300 men* took on the huge array of Midianites, victory required an absolute *miracle.*

When *Naaman* dipped in the Jordan River to receive healing of his leprosy, it took a *miracle* for the healing to occur.

When the *wine* ran out at the marriage in Cana, it took a *miracle* of Jesus for the water in the water pots to turn into wine.

When the *widow of Zarephath* was eating her last meal, it required a *miracle* for it to multiply. *God never gives you a Dream that does not require His participation.*

The Uncommon Dream will not happen without your constant awareness that it will take the hand of God to make it happen.

God will never involve Himself in a Dream that you can accomplish *alone.*

The purpose of every single act of God is to increase your dependency upon Him and your addiction to His presence.

12 Keys To Unlock Miracles For Your Dreams

1.   Recognize The Uncommon Dream You Desire Will Require Miracles From God. *You will not succeed alone.*

2.   Expect Miracles In Your Life Daily. "For he that cometh to God must believe that He is, and that He is a rewarder of them that diligently seek Him," (Hebrews 11:6).

3.   Remember Miracles Will Require A Continuous Flow Of Faith. "But without faith it is impossible to please Him," (Hebrews 11:6).

4.   Feed Your Faith—Confidence In God. It enters your heart when you hear the words of God spoken.   "So then faith cometh by hearing, and hearing by the word of God," (Romans 10:17).

5.   Understand That The Logic Of Your Mind And The Faith Of Your Heart Collide. They will wage war with each other continually as you search to discover and achieve your Dream. "For the flesh lusteth against the Spirit, and the Spirit against the flesh: and these are contrary the one to the other: so that ye cannot do the things that ye would do. But the fruit of the Spirit is...faith," (Galatians 5:17, 22).

6.   Logic Produces Order; Faith Produces Miracles.   God will never consult your logic to determine your future. *He permits your faith to* *determine the levels of your promotion and victories.*

7. Logic Is The Wonderful And Valuable Gift He Gives You To Create Order In Your Dealings With People.

8. Faith Is The Wonderful And Valuable Gift He Gives You To Create Miracles... Through The Father.

9. The Fulfillment Of The Uncommon Dream Will Require Miracle Relationships With Mentors, Protegés, Friends And Golden Connections. For example, Joseph would never have entered the palace without the miracle relationship with the butler, *a Divine Connection.*

10. The Uncommon Dream May Require Supernatural Financial Provision. For example, Peter experienced the miracle of the coin in the mouth of the fish to pay his taxes. *Financial miracles are normal in the lives of those who obey God.*

11. The Uncommon Dream Will Require The Miracle Of Wisdom. Your decisions will open doors or close doors. *Each decision you make will decrease you or increase you.*

12. Miracles Come Easily To The Obedient. "If ye be willing and obedient, ye shall eat the good of the land," (Isaiah 1:19).

Any Move Toward Self-Sufficiency Is A Move Away From God. You must cultivate continuous gratefulness and thankfulness in your heart for the presence of The Holy Spirit. *Check His countenance. Pursue His approval.* "The Lord make His face shine upon thee, and be gracious unto thee: The Lord lift up His countenance upon thee, and give thee peace," (Numbers 6:25-26).

Remember, Your Dream Will Require Miracles.

Wrong Dreams Become Substitutes For The Right Dreams. It is very important that you do not pursue a Dream or Goal that God did not instruct you to pursue. When you pursue something God did not instruct you to have, He is not obligated to sustain you *emotionally, physically or financially.*

Anything You Pursue Alone Will Fail.

After David had conquered his enemies, he was sitting in his house. He indicated to Nathan, the prophet, that he wanted to build a special house for God. The prophet immediately responded, "Go, do all that is in thine heart; for the Lord is with thee," (2 Samuel 7:3).

Even Prophets Can Be Wrong When They Fail To Consult God. That evening God spoke to Nathan to bring a special word to David. David was not to build the house of the Lord.

Rather, God had established that David's Seed would do so instead. "I will set up thy seed after thee, which shall proceed out of thy bowels, and I will establish his kingdom. He shall build an house for My name," (2 Samuel 7:12-13). Mentors often see the future of their protegés years in advance.

Never exclude The Holy Spirit from your pursuit of His Dream in your life.

The Uncommon Dream Requires Supernatural Intervention.

～ 17 ～
THE UNCOMMON DREAM MUST BE CLEARLY DEFINED AND CONTINUOUSLY REFINED

Strength Is The Product Of Focus.

Have you decided The Dream for your life? It cannot be something suggested by friends or family or anyone else. It cannot be your Mother's Dream.

The Uncommon Dream Will Create The Uncommon Life. It Must Be Your Own Dream.

Who Are You Learning From?

What Are You Learning From Them?

What Are You Presently Learning?

Is Your Learning Related To Your Dream?

Your learning needs to be connected to your passion. ***You Can Only Do...What You See Internally And Outwardly.***

The Uncommon Dream Will Require Time. The Uncommon Dream must become so important, that it dominates every conversation.

Have you ever heard a mother talking excitedly about a baby soon to be born? You might start talking about someone named Bill. She interrupts with, "Bill, that is a good name. That is a good name for this baby." Then you start talking about The United

Nations and the same mother-to-be says, "Oh, I hope he does go around the world someday. That would be wonderful!"

What has happened? *That baby is the Mother's Dream and is the only topic important in her mind.*

Your Dream Must Grow. That is how you know a Dream is from God. It is *designed...stirred* and is *growing*.

▶ *How much Time are you willing to invest daily in your Dream?*

▶ *How much Money are you willing to invest?*

▶ *How much Effort are you willing to invest toward your Dream?*

▶ *Who has helped you and inspired you to achieve your Dream?*

▶ *Who are the people that need to be inspired to be involved in your Dream?*

▶ *Whose Dream are you helping to fulfill?*

Friends are shaping and sculpturing what you value. When you have a Dream, identify those who consistently believe in you.

The Quality Of Your Uncommon Dream Does Not Guarantee The Fulfillment Of Your Dream. Adolf Hitler had a horrible Dream, things he wanted to destroy. Unfortunately, he achieved those dreams. You can have a worthy Dream and still never achieve it. You can focus on an evil Dream and obtain it. Divine laws work for everyone.

You Must Define Your Dream, Refine It And Confine Your Life To It.

▶ *God Had A Dream...in Adam.*

▶ *Martin Luther King Had A Dream... bring deliverance to his people.*

► *Joseph* Had A Dream...*sustain others during a famine.*

► *Jesus* Had A Dream...*to seek and save that which was lost.* Jesus "...for the joy that was set before Him endured the cross," (Hebrews 12:2).

The picture you keep looking at determines the strength that enters you.

What Picture Dominates Your Mind?

God desires to work in you.

He is watching you...observing you, and has a great interest in your success in life. "That He would grant you, according to the riches of His glory, to be strengthened with might by His Spirit in the inner man; That Christ may dwell in your hearts by faith; that ye, being rooted and grounded in love, May be able to comprehend with all saints what is the breadth, and length, and depth, and height; And to know the love of Christ, which passeth knowledge, that ye might be filled with all the fulness of God," (Ephesians 3:16-19).

Your Success Is God's Dream!

God wants you to have an understanding of His plan, His intentions toward you. God is so interested in your life that He can exceed what you are thinking about. He can *even* exceed the desires of your heart. "Now unto him who is able to do exceeding abundantly above all that we ask or think, according to the power that worketh in us," (Ephesians 3:20).

Your Focus Creates Strength

There was a little girl trapped beneath the

weight of a 1,500-pound car. Her mother lifted the car off of her. Later, the mother was unable to lift even 200 pounds. But, her child had been under the car. *She was able to lift that car because her child was her focus.* Strength is not the product of a muscle; it is the product of a focus.

Every satanic strategy in your life is to break your focus on God.

The Uncommon Dream Is An Invisible Picture Of Your Future. Example: Jesus, for the joy that was set before Him, endured the cross. Jesus did not go to the cross; *He went through the cross, to the resurrection.* The photograph in the mind of Christ was not, "I am going to the cross." In His mind...He went through the crucifixion, to the resurrection, and now He is at the right hand of the throne of God. *The picture of His reward... you and me...enabled Him to endure the tortuous ordeal of The Cross.*

I cannot change what is in your hand, until I can change what is in your head. The picture is what carries you through to fulfill every Dream God has given you.

I cannot change your provisions, until I change your photograph. I have to change the picture, what you keep seeing controls what you feel.

Power Facts To Remember

You will not change your life until you change the vision. Whatever you keep seeing on the inside of you, is what your faith will operate on.

Vision, Faith And Doubts

▶ Your Vision Is Your Future.

▶ Faith Has To Have A Photograph.

▶ Faith Must Be In The One Who Gave You That Dream.

▶ Faith Must Be In The One Who Is The Miracle Worker.

▶ Faith Must Be In Who Can Make Your Dream A Reality.

▶ Doubt Is Faith In Your Adversary.

▶ Doubt Is Just As Powerful As Faith.

▶ Doubt Does Not Delay Miracles.

▶ Doubt Produces Tragedy.

▶ Doubt Must Not Be Allowed To Become Greater Than Your Faith.

▶ Doubt Is Merely Another Word For Faith In Your Enemy.

▶ Doubt Schedules Tragedies As Quickly As Faith Schedules Miracles.

Giants Or Grapes

Remember the Biblical story of Moses sending spies to investigate Canaan? Twelve spies were sent to Canaan. Two of the spies believed they could take the enemies of the land. Joshua and Caleb believed they could take the giants. *Ten of the spies doubted...* saw the giants bigger than the grapes. They saw giants bigger than God was. They compared the giants with themselves.

Joshua and Caleb compared God with the giants and said, "We can take the country."

You will face enemies while endeavoring to create and accomplish your Dream.

What Is Your Dream? *What do you want? It is hard to define clearly, what you want.* It must be something you believe God wants you to achieve. You can feed it or starve it. You can grow it or ignore it. The directions you pursue reveal *The Dream* that has consumed you.

▶ Define Your Dream...*Be Fully Persuaded In Your Own Mind.* Can you picture your Dream?

▶ Refine Your Dream...*Through Planning Daily Goals.*

▶ Confine Your Dream...*Give Your Whole Life To Your Dream.* Resist anything that distracts from it. Look for reasons to succeed...not reasons to fail. *Your Uncommon Dream is waiting for fulfillment.*

The Uncommon Dream Must Be Continuously Defined And Refined To Become A Reality.

❦ 18 ❦

THE UNCOMMON DREAM WILL REQUIRE UNCOMMON PASSION

Passion Is Intense Energized Desire.

13 Exciting Facts About Passion

1. **Passion Is A Current.** *It decides what comes toward you or moves away from you.*

Water has currents.

Air has currents.

Passion creates currents in life.

2. **Passion Is An Irresistible Magnet That Pulls Others Toward You To Participate.** Focus births passion. Feed it and it will become strong desire. Feed it continuously and it will become an obsession.

3. **Passion Creates Favor.** *Currents of Favor* flow toward the person who is passionate and confident toward their Dream.

Remember Wisdom Key #115: *Currents Of Favor Begin To Flow The Moment That You Solve A Problem For Someone.*

4. **Your Passion Decides Who Is Comfortable With You.** *If you are passionate... your persuasion will be evident.* You are responsible to

generate excitement in others to get them involved with your Dream. The persuaded *persuade.*

Those close to you will fuel your fire. They will follow your passion and celebrate your focus. *However, they will need reminding and encouragement.* Those around you are meditating on their own failures. They have doubts about themselves. They may lack certainty and clarity concerning their own dreams.

5. Your Passion Intimidates Any Potential Mountain In Your Path. When you face their mountain of collected memories...you must use your passion *as a drilling tool, a hot iron, a welder's instrument* to pierce those barriers.

Tell them about your Dream...*repeatedly.*

6. Your Passion Can Unlock Dormant Passion In Others. You see...deep inside of those you love...there is a hope that you will be the one who helps them to break the cycle of tragedy and loss in their own life. They want you to win more than you realize. *They want you to be an example to follow.* Others are watching. They hate their own losses...*the cycle of mediocrity.*

They will test you because they do not want to lean on something that will *falter, stumble* and *fail again.* They are hoping you will stand strong. Many think that everybody wants you to fail. In fact, I heard a public speaker say recently, "Most people want you to fail...very few want you to win." I *disagree.*

7. Passion Distinguishes You From The Crowd. Multitudes are pursuing heroes. When you are watching television you are most likely identifying with the hero, the champion...you want him to win!

Others want you to win...especially those closest to you. Stand strong...follow your Dream with passion. *Be relentless in pursuit of your Dream.*

8. Passion Is The Seed Commanded To Your Environment. Success requires energy. It requires energy to move toward your goals... regardless of your circumstances, your feelings, or obstacles.

9. The Passion Gap Explains Failed Marriages. *Passion will always put a distance between you and those without it.* Guard your passion. Passion is your greatest weapon.

10. Passion Decides The Speed Of Your Learning. Passion decides what you are willing to study...willing to pursue...willing to endure.

11. Passion Is The Aura That Attracts Good People. Life always opens the door widest to the passionate people with purpose. Here is the story of friends of mine from Tampa, Florida. They went to Florida with nothing.

There were about 100 people in the church. I spoke at their first banquet. Recently, a woman gave them a $400,000 building...they have been blessed with explosive favor. Today two thousand people worship together as they are reaching the inner cities of Tampa, Florida.

12. Passion Is Irresistible. *Become so passionate about your Dream that it becomes an obsession.* You will create an atmosphere and climate around you that others cannot resist.

13. Passion Exposes Weakness And Forces Its Submission To Your Dream. *Passion Penetrates And Controls Any Environment.* Those who are weak without purpose will *feel your passion.* Those who have a passion themselves... *will respect your passion.*

4 Ways To Increase Your Passion

1. Unclutter Your Life Of Anything That Does Not Belong In It. You cannot do everything. Unclutter your life...by uncluttering your day. Schedule fewer appointments. Choose your friends wisely. Never write a letter when a phone call can accomplish the same result. Never make a phone call...that someone else can make for you.

2. Determine The Purpose Of Each Relationship Near You. Some have pursued you...*for something you do not have.* Identify time-wasters. Identify the parasites that only want what you have *earned*...instead of what you have *learned.*

Friendliness Is Not Friendship. You cannot be friends with everybody. *Do not feed friendships that weaken your enthusiasm for your Dream.*

3. Treasure And Protect Your Personal Health. Fatigue is an enemy to a Dream. One of the great presidents refused to make a decision after 3:00 p.m. every day. He had recognized that when he was tired, he assessed things *differently...usually wrong.*

4. Create An Environment That Feeds Your Passion For Your Dream. The happiest church office I have ever entered belongs to my dear friend in Sarasota, Florida. His office is like a museum! Children rush into his office every Sunday night...just to view the aquarium, the toys, and the many items that make you "smile." He said, "Anything that makes me laugh, I put it around me…to keep my spirits up."

Protect Your Passion.
Men Do Not Decide Their Dreams.
Men Discover Their Dreams.
Men Do Not Choose Their Passion.
Their Passion Chooses Them.

3 Enemies Of Your Passion

There will be enemies against *every goal in your life.* You must recognize them.

1.   Fatigue…When you are tired, you do not see a good future. When you get tired…you start talking in a negative manner. You say the wrong things. Your words become walls instead of doors.

Fatigue Is An Enemy To Passion.

2.   Double-Mindedness…"I am not sure this is something I am *suppose* to do." These words will dilute and create doubt.

3.   Doubt Is An Enemy To Your Passion. The best cure for doubt is information. Discover all you can about your Dream and Passion.

The Uncommon Dream Will Require Uncommon Passion.

Your Words
Are The Seeds
For Feelings.

-MIKE MURDOCK

❧ 19 ❧

THE UNCOMMON DREAM IS KEPT ALIVE WITH SPOKEN WORDS

━━━━⟫•◆•⟪━━━━

Your Words Are The Seeds For Feelings.
Your conversations need to amplify your Dream. Your words can easily dilute the Dream if you are talking opposite of your desired future.

God has given you a *Mouth* and a *Mind* to *magnify* your strength, to *increase* your capability.

You cannot lose weight by expressing negative statements, "I just see a menu and I start getting bigger," or "I gain weight just looking at food."

Your words should reflect your desires...reflect your confidence in your Dream. You schedule for failure with negative thoughts and words.

The Basketball Phenomenon

A Famous University did an incredible test showing the power of the mind. I studied it for two years. It is *incredible*. It is *powerful*.

Two basketball teams were selected, A and B. For 30 consecutive days, team A was instructed to practice free throws in the gym for one hour a day...for 30 days.

Team B was told to sit in the locker room, and

visualize themselves standing at the free throw line shooting free throws. Team B was instructed to *picture the ball going through the net.* Team B was not allowed to touch the ball. They could not be on the ball court. They were allowed to see the ball *only in their mind.*

At the end of 30 days, Team A, who had been out in the gym practicing free throws 30 days, one hour a day...had increased their average by 22 percent.

Team B had not touched a ball in 30 days...*had only visualized the ball going through the net*...their percentage rose 21 percent—*almost identical* to those who had practiced with the actual basketball.

Your Mind Has Everything To Do With Your Energy, Your Focus. If satan defeats you...*it will be through your mind and your words.*

You win or lose...according to how you control your mind...your thoughts. "As he thinketh in his heart, so is he," (Proverbs 23:7).

What Happens Inside You Affects What Happens Around You. Stop seeing yourself as a loser, poor, broke, ignorant and unable to achieve what you desire. If that happens in your mind, every other part of your body will cooperate.

The Football Phenomenon

A phenomenal thing happened with a certain football team. An experiment was performed to discover what the effect of words would do to the mind *according to what was believed.*

The players were told they had been exposed to bacteria in their system...a disease. They were required to go to the hospital for tests.

In one week it was reported that two of the players were paralyzed and could not get out of bed. One had severe ringing in his ears and a variety of symptoms was evident. As they reviewed the list of players...it appeared there was *something wrong with every one of them*.

The mysterious truth was...*NOTHING was wrong with any of them*. There was no bacteria in their bodies...no disease. It was a research to discover *power of* **WORDS**...*the power of Suggestion...the power of* **VISUALIZATION.**

When **WORD-PICTURES** were planted into their minds of what could be wrong in their bodies...*the body cooperated with the mind and produced the anticipated symptoms.*

Your Own Words Are Affecting Your Self-Portrait. They give you a clear picture of the YOU in your future...*the picture God is looking at.* When God sees you, what does He say to the angels? Does He smile? What does He do? What does He say?

Say What God Says About You In His Word.

Words Are Not Cheap. "He that hath knowledge spareth his words: and a man of understanding is of an excellent spirit. Even a fool, when he holdeth his peace, is counted wise: and he that shutteth his lips is esteemed a man of understanding," (Proverbs 17:27-28).

Wars begin because of words. Peace comes when great men *come together*, *negotiate* and *dialogue*.

7 Keys About The Power Of Words

1. **Any Man Who Controls His Mouth Is Literally Protecting His Own Life.** "He that

keepeth his mouth keepeth his life," (Proverbs 13:3).

2. Those Who Talk Too Much Will Eventually Be Destroyed. "He that openeth wide his lips shall have destruction," (Proverbs 13:3).

3. Right Words Can Turn An Angry Man Into A Friend, And Wrong Words Can Turn A Friend Into An Enemy. "A soft answer turneth away wrath: but grievous words stir up anger," (Proverbs 15:1).

4. Wisdom Is Necessary In Order To Speak The Right Words. "The heart of the wise teacheth his mouth, and addeth learning to his lips," (Proverbs 16:23).

5. Your Words Reveal Whether You Are Wise Or A Fool. "The tongue of the wise useth knowledge aright: but the mouth of fools poureth out foolishness," (Proverbs 15:2).

6. The Purpose Of Words Is To Educate, Enthuse And Energize Those Around You. "The lips of the wise disperse knowledge," (Proverbs 15:7).

7. Wrong Words Create Heart Wounds That Make Trust Impossible. "The words of a talebearer are as wounds, and they go down into the innermost parts of the belly," (Proverbs 18:8).

Do Not Allow Your Words To Destroy Your Dream! Jesus said your words reveal what kind of heart you possess, "For of the abundance of the heart his mouth speaketh," (Luke 6:45).

Words Created The World. (See Genesis 1.)

Words Create Your World.

Words Link People.

Words Are The Bridge To Your Future.

There is a time to talk...a time to listen...a time

for movement…a time for staying still. "Death and life are in the power of the tongue: and they that love it shall eat the fruit thereof," (Proverbs 18:21).

When people were hungry for knowledge, Jesus spoke for hours. When He got to Pontius Pilate's hall, His truth was ignored and He was silent.

Silence Speaks

Stay Silent In Revealing The Damage An Enemy Has Done.

Stay Silent In Discussing Weaknesses Of Others.

Stay Silent In Advertising Your Own Mistakes.

Jesus knew when to talk and when to listen.

You can learn too. It will benefit you in every way as you endeavor to discover and develop your Dream.

Ask The Holy Spirit to guard your tongue and your words…to teach you to listen and speak with Wisdom.

The Uncommon Dream Is Kept Alive With Spoken Words.

Someone Is Always
Observing You
Who Is Capable
Of Greatly Blessing You.

-*MIKE MURDOCK*

❧ 20 ❧

THE UNCOMMON DREAM WILL REQUIRE UNCOMMON FAVOR

———➤•❂•◀———

Favor Is When Others Desire To Bless You.

An Uncommon Dream will require an unusual amount of Favor from many different people. You must realize the importance of Favor.

15 Unforgettable Facts About Favor

1. True Favor Is A Gift From God Through People. You must recognize Favor as something you really do not deserve. Now, in the business world, talk often revolves around, "He owes me a favor."

A Favor...Is Much Different Than Favor.

A favor is an act of kindness designed to *control, manipulate,* or *compensate* you for something. I believe you will always resent someone you owe. Refuse relationships of indebtedness. When someone tells you that another person owes them a favor, be weary and cautious.

2. Gratitude Is A Magnet For Favor. A dear friend of mine has said many times, "What you are most thankful for will increase in your life." *When you do not value the good will and contribution of others...it will stop.*

Your Dream will require Uncommon Favor. Somebody is talking about you right now *favorably*.

3. Favor Is When Someone Creates Access Upward. There are people that The Holy Spirit is directing to give gifts to you, to bless you...to open doors that will create access for you.

4. Favor Is When Someone Prays For Your Success. *Your Dream will require Intercessors who greatly influence the flow of Favor in your life.* When you truly respect intercession, you will see the most dramatic results you have ever experienced in your lifetime.

5. Favor Is When Someone Recognizes Your Intense Efforts. Your struggles and efforts are noted. Someone is carefully evaluating your *progress*, *pursuits* and *potential*. The observations of Boaz birthed his marriage with Ruth (Ruth 1-4).

6. Favor Can Begin In The Heart Of Someone You Do Not Yet Know. You may not even know the person. It would astound you if you knew who is discussing you with great Favor and appreciation.

7. Favor Is Always A Reward For Faithfulness. Your *consistency* is attracting attention. Your ability to *stay focused* is like a magnet. Someone is observing you and considering entering your life with *favor, influence* and *support*. You will have access to their *skills, Wisdom* and circle of *friendships*.

8. Favor Overflows Around Integrity. Others are admiring your *endurance*. The observation of your *integrity* would amaze and thrill you.

9. Favor Creates Quick Success. When

favor enters your life, you will achieve in a single day what would normally require a year to accomplish alone.

10. Favor Is Always Proportionate To Your Diligence. Someone is observing your productivity and attitude toward your present boss and superior.

11. An Uncommon Attitude Always Generates An Unexplainable Flow Of Favor. *It happened to Ruth.* She was a *lonely*, *focused* and *loyal* peasant woman who was trying to find enough food to survive. *Someone noticed her.* Boaz, the wealthy landowner, came to review the Harvest. He approached Ruth after inquiring about her to his supervisors. Her humility and sweet spirit touched Boaz. He explained that he knew about her and that provision would be there as long as she wanted to reap in his field.

12. Favor Must Become Your Seed Into Others. *Every good Seed that you have sown is going to bear fruit and grow.* Every hour you have invested in restoring and healing others will produce an incredible Harvest.

13. Favor Is Always Seasonal. *Your sacrifices are not in vain.* Your toil and struggles have been *noted*, *documented* and *observed* by the Lord of the Harvest! "And let us not be weary in well doing: for in due season we shall reap, if we faint not," (Galatians 6:9).

This kind of Favor always follows those who are *excited, focused* and *obsessed* with their Dream.

14. Favor Always Has A Divine Purpose. God goes before you. He places inside the hearts of others the desire to *aid* you, to *assist* you and *enable* you to bring your Dream to completion.

Others observe how you solve problems...how you respond to adversity and difficulty.

15. Success Increases Favor. *It happened in the life of Paul.* He was shipwrecked on the island of Melita. Paul had gathered a bundle of sticks and laid them on the fire. A snake came out of the fire and fastened onto his hand. The barbarians of the island talked among themselves. They thought, "No doubt this man is a murderer, whom, though he hath escaped the sea, yet vengeance suffereth not to live," (Acts 28:4). Nevertheless, Paul shook off the snake into the fire, and felt no harm.

That anointing for *conquering* affected those watching. Their minds were changed and said, "He must be a god!"

Overcoming talks. Others around you observe your life. Others will learn from you as they observe your life...your *focus, victories* and *endurance.*

Investors study young couples. They observe their aggressiveness and pursuit of excellence before investing.

Leaders scrutinize and note behavior of the assistants of fellow leaders.

Powerful men long for someone to trust...to work beside them daily.

Aggressive leaders search continually for others who are *aggressive, energized and diligent.*

Pursue excellence in your present circumstances. Whatever your Dream may be, *empty your best efforts into it.*

Do not wait for a glorious future to arrive... pursue it with enthusiasm. Your rewards will be greater than you ever dreamed.

Picture this: You are running on the track of life. The grandstands of spectators are observing you—far more than you could possibly know. "Wherefore seeing we also are compassed about with so great a cloud of witnesses, let us lay aside every weight, and the sin which doth so easily beset us, and let us run with patience the race that is set before us," (Hebrews 12:1).

Run with excellence. Remember: *Someone Is Always Observing You Who Is Capable Of Greatly Blessing You With Favor.*

The Uncommon Dream Will Require Uncommon Favor.

Your Future Is Decided
By What You
Are Willing To Change.

-MIKE MURDOCK

∽ 21 ∽

THE UNCOMMON DREAM DETERMINES WHAT YOU BECOME WILLING TO CHANGE

Your Future Will Necessitate Change.

God reminds us through the prophet Isaiah: "Behold, *I will do a new thing*; now it shall spring forth; shall ye not know it? I will even make a way in the wilderness, and rivers in the desert," (Isaiah 43:19).

Trust The Holy Spirit to enable and empower you to change. Know why change is necessary.

Ask Mentors for advice and counsel in changes they see you should make. Be willing to take small daily steps toward change.

The Holy Spirit is the One who can initiate those changes and the people who can help you to change.

The Holy Spirit arranges people in your life to help you change...to see what you do not see...to know what you do not know.

Some changes will not happen *instantly*. It will be progressively. God does not give you all the information at one time.

The Holy Spirit Is The Agent Of Change. I not only want to be changed, but, I want to be a Changer.

I want someone to say to me, "You have unlocked something in me and I will never be the same...You have created a miracle in my life."

Embrace change. Be willing to move into the next season of your life. Your Uncommon Dream will require changes in your life. Are you willing to make them?

You hear it said constantly, "You cannot change anybody." I disagree. We marry to create change... friends create change.

My father brought a phenomenal truth to my attention. He said if I walk in the light that I presently have, I would receive more light...as a Divine reward.

When I see someone, who refuses to change... it is more than a *Wisdom problem. It is also a rebellion problem.*

If they were walking in the light they have, they would be receiving more light. Think on this.

Are you walking in the light that you know?

Are there changes you need to make?

Your Circumstances Are Created By Your Decisions. Your Decisions Are The Product Of Your Wisdom.

I can predict your future by your willingness to change.

We read the story of Peter and Judas. They had access to the same Savior and knowledge from the same source. *One was willing to change. One was not willing to change. Peter was willing to change...Judas was not.*

Your mind requires renewing *(changing)* every day. I constantly need change. Nobody really likes the word change…yet we must be willing to change.

The unwillingness to change has consequences.

Pain…if you do not change. Pain is always the presence of loss.

Pleasure…is the product of gain…requiring change.

Remember Wisdom Key #89: *Pain Is The Proof Of Disorder.*

Change means you must do something that you are not presently doing. "If ye be willing and obedient, ye shall eat the good of the land: But if ye refuse and rebel, ye shall be devoured with the sword: for the mouth of the Lord hath spoken it," (Isaiah 1:19-20).

Change also means…you must stop doing something that you are comfortable doing.

Change May Cause Pain For The Present, But Gain For The Future.

The Uncommon Dream requires many changes in *Relationship, Habits, Patterns and Schedules.*

Not once does God assume that somebody is not capable of change. He continuously attributed lack of change to *ignorance or rebellion.* "My people are destroyed for lack of knowledge," (Hosea 4:6).

Ignorance can be a source of pain. *If you are willing to change…the pain can eventually be pleasure.*

10 Reasons People Resist Change

1. The Change Is Not Self-Initiated. Something was not their idea. They feel like they are being manipulated. The solution is to allow others to have input and feel like they are part of the change process.

2. Routine Is Disrupted. Routine is a group-learned reaction we do repeatedly without much thought. Change threatens our habit patterns forcing us to think and re-evaluate.

3. Change Creates Fear Of The Unknown. Change means we may have to do things we have never done before. This causes our insecurities to rise.

4. The Purpose Of Change May Be Unclear. We hear about the change from a second-hand source. In addition, we need an explanation, a prompt and clear understanding.

5. Change May Create A Fear Of Failure. Not being sure of what lies ahead or of the unknown. People hold on to what feels comfortable.

6. Change Will Not Happen When People Engage In Negative Thinking And Behavior. You can do anything if you put your mind and focus on it.

7. Distrust Of Leadership. When followers do not like the leader who oversees the changes needed, their feelings will not allow them to look at the changes objectively.

8. Feelings Of Insignificance And Unworthiness. A person may feel that the change is a personal attack.

9. Change May Mean Personal Loss. Everyone ask this question when there is a change. How will this affect me? Most of the time there are three groups affected by change.

Those Who *Lose*.

Those Who *Are Not* Affected.

Those Who *Will Benefit*.

10. True Change Always Requires Additional Commitment. More of your *time...* more of your *responsibility...*more *commitment*.

Your Willingness To Change Will Determine The Reality, The Outcome And The Quality Of Your Uncommon Dream.

Prayer For Inner Change. "Holy Spirit, *I want to change.* I want everything unholy in me to be uprooted. I want what is *right* to grow inside of me. I expect it in the name of Jesus. Amen."

The Uncommon Dream Determines What You Become Willing To Change.

RECOMMENDED FOR YOUR WISDOM LIBRARY:
B-14   Seeds of Wisdom on Relationships, Vol. 2 (32 pages/$3)
B-98   The Assignment: The Pain & The Passion
        (144 pages/$10)
B-100   The Holy Spirit Handbook, Vol. 1 (153 pages/$10)

Patience Is The Weapon
That Forces Deception
To Reveal Itself.

-MIKE MURDOCK

∿ 22 ∿
THE UNCOMMON DREAM WILL REQUIRE UNCOMMON PATIENCE

━━▶⊱⊙⊰◀━━

Patience Is Mastery Of The Present.

10 Facts You Should Know About Patience

1.   Your Patience Is A Sign Of Trust. "The Lord is good unto them that wait for Him, to the soul that seeketh Him," (Lamentations 3:25). "It is good that a man should both hope and quietly wait for the salvation of the Lord," (Lamentations 3:26).

2.   Patience Is A Seed.   It is the season between sowing and reaping. That is why the Bible calls it Seed-Time and Harvest. Time is the season between the Seed and the Harvest.

3.   Patience Is Often Burdensome. You may have lost the joy of your Dream because of the waiting. It breeds *agitation*, a *critical* spirit and leaves you *frustrated*.

4.   Your Patience In Waiting May Be Painful. When you are *waiting*...sometimes wrong words are spoken that *abort* the cycle of blessing. You must refuse to permit words of discouragement in your mouth. "Fear thou not; for I am with thee: be not dismayed; for I am thy God: I will strengthen thee;

yea, I will help thee; yea, I will uphold thee with the right hand of My righteousness," (Isaiah 41:10).

5. Patience Authorizes God To Confront Your Adversaries. The Holy Spirit is involved against the enemies of your Dream. Every *scheme, strategy* and *trap* against you shall ultimately fail if you are patient in waiting.

6. Patience Documents Your Expectations Of God. Keep your eyes on the rewards of your Patience...*the reality of your Dream...it will come to pass.* Never give up. Never quit. Overcoming involves more than one battle.

7. Patience Always Decides The Outcome. The individual that refuses to quit will win and accomplish The Uncommon Dream he desires.

8. Patience Is Continually Produced By Continuous Praise. *Unthankfulness can bring a curse, not a blessing.* While you are waiting, create a climate of thanksgiving and gratitude. "In every thing give thanks: for this is the will of God in Christ Jesus concerning you," (1 Thessalonians 5:18).

9. Remember Patience Always Produces A Favorable Response From God. *Waiting is very difficult.*

The Holy Spirit is keenly aware of every emotional upheaval you may have at this moment. Sometimes your pain comes from simply refusing to be patient and wait for God's timing. *Our God is glorious! He is watching you.* Nothing escapes His attention. For the ungodly, this may seem unsettling...that they are watched. *For the person that wants the will of God... this is a delight.*

10. Patience Is A Weapon.

Patience Is The Weapon That Forces Deception To Reveal Itself. It exposes hidden deceit. "For the vision is yet for an appointed time, but at the end it shall speak and not lie: though it tarry, wait for it; because it will surely come, it will not tarry," (Habakkuk 2:3).

5 Keys That Develop Patience

1. **Remember That Time Will Expose What Interrogation Cannot.** Think of relationships in your past. Remember your first impressions? Time proved differently in many cases. First impressions are not always correct.

2. **View Time As Your Friend.** Permit it to work in your life and relationships. It will force facts to emerge that the greatest interrogator on earth could not expose. "To every thing there is a season, and a time to every purpose under the heaven," (Ecclesiastes 3:1).

3. **Focus On The Completion Of Present Tasks.** There are many unfinished things around you. Complete those items while you are waiting for other information and decisions. Stay productive.

Master the art of completion. *It is best to become a Finisher...rather than simply a Starter.*

4. **Review The Stories Of Successful Champions Who Have Understood The Power Of Patience.** Thomas Edison experimented 5,000 times with one invention. When asked how he felt about so many failures, he replied that he had not failed, he had only "discovered something that would not work." *Absorb the success stories of others. It will affect your confidence and breathe energy and endurance into you.*

5. **Remind Yourself Of The Losses**

Impatience Has Always Created. Impatience is deadly. It destroys the birth of that which is great and good. I remember reading the story of a little chick that was trying to peck its way out of its eggshell. A little farmer's daughter decided to "help it." She broke the egg open...*the chick died.*

The *patient* pecking of the little chick was developing strength for its entry into the world. The *waiting* gave it time to grow its own strength. When the little girl broke the egg...*it was too soon.*

Impatience causes you to speak too quickly, saying words that do not edify. This also grieves The Holy Spirit delaying your Dream from coming to pass.

The Uncommon Dream Will Require Uncommon Patience.

❧ 23 ❧
THE UNCOMMON DREAM WILL REQUIRE GOOD HEALTH AND ENERGY

———————◆———————

Good Health Habits Generate Joy.
Mind, body and spirit need renewing...daily.
Do not expect miracles to compensate for ignorance. We will stand in line for one hour for the prayer of healing but refuse to jog for five minutes.

Our own decisions have often created our health problems.

You will not feel good towards God if you do not feel good about yourself. Two things did not change when you accepted Christ into your heart...*your mind and your body.*

Your mind needs renewing daily with The Word of God.

Your body must be disciplined daily... with exercise.

What You Do Daily Determines What You Will Do Permanently.

18 Power Thoughts About Good Health

1. Health Is More Important Than Healing. Some ministers have not yet seen the value of encouraging their congregations to pursue good health habits.

2.   Your Body Is A Divine Gift; Your Care Of It Is Proof Of Gratitude. We are responsible to take care of what God has given us. It is a challenge. *It will always be a challenge...but a worthy goal.*

3.   Any Action Toward Health Generates Joy. Every day you move toward health, you will increase your joy and your peace. *When there is joy and peace...*there is *motivation* and *focus* to follow the steps to your Dream.

4.   Buy The Wisdom Of A Fitness Trainer. *Weights can be used daily.* When possible...secure a trainer to get you started. They will know exactly what you need for your body type and motivate you as no one else can.

Find a *personal trainer* who knows how to help you get to where you want to go in the shortest amount of time.

Remind yourself of the advantages and benefits of strength and having a strong body. Learn the secrets about weight lifting...and strength training.

Subscribe to weight lifting magazines that help you *visualize* your future success and the changes in your body.

5.   Schedule Your Morning Health Hour. Workout...*personalize your own physical workout.* When I have been traveling for hours...I do not feel like exercising when I get home...but the rewards are worth it when I do.

Watch videos while you work out. Watch the results of your life and your body as you will begin to see changes if you are consistent.

6. Place Visual Pictures Around You That Birth Motivation And Expectation.

Expect *patiently instead of grumbling and whining when you do not see immediate results.*

Expect God to do His supernatural part in responding to your pursuit for health.

Expect your body to make the necessary changes. You did not get where you are instantly and you will not regain what you want instantly.

7. Walk One Mile A Day. Walking... *twenty minutes to an hour a day can revolutionize your life... your emotions...your focus.* Walk...*tall like a champion with your shoulders back.*

Walk...*with a picture of health in your mind.* Walk...*expecting radical improvement.* Walk...*tall like a weight-lifter or Olympic champion.* Keep this picture in your mind.

Walk...*with imagination, as if you are in a contest and you are ahead of everyone else.* Walk...*with a purpose and goal in your mind...*for instance, take this time to memorize a Scripture or listen to a one-hour teaching tape as you walk.

Listen to Scriptures with your headphones. Walking is the best exercise to radically, positively affect your mood swings...*the way you think.*

Walking prevents lower back pain. The benefits of a good walking routine are too numerous to mention in this chapter.

Become conscious of your time. Remember you are sowing into your whole future...*perfect health.*

Watch losers deteriorate before your eyes because they took their health lightly or for granted. They *used to be* champions.

Maybe as you read this, you are saying, "*It is too late for me!*"

No! It is not too late! You can begin again and still be *a Winner...a Champion.*

Read these chapters again...*begin to apply personal changes.* New results will soon be yours.

*Pursue with diligence to develop a body that pleases God...*one of good health and energy. At the same time, your new health habits will aid you in accomplishing your Dream. *Good Health Takes Time With Consistent Good Habits.*

8. Pursue Health Habits Openly And Aggressively. Be ruthless in asserting your posture and purpose in *developing* good health. *Note that when you discuss losing weight, that is when they offer you donuts!*

9. Everything In Your Life Is A Habit. What new *health habit* will benefit your Dream?

10. Change Your Health One Day At A Time. *What is one thing you can change today toward your new healthy lifestyle?* Develop the habit of health consciousness. You do not have to have a handful of keys to start your car...*just one.*

11. Romance Your Body Through Self-Talk. Positive Self-Talk *will encourage you when no one else can.* Look at your body and say, "You are a gift from God to me. I am going to do my best to protect your *heart*...your *mind* and *increase your strength* by what I say and do. I am going to take care of you."

Talk to yourself. Talk good health options to others. What you talk about will increase in your life. You will move towards anything you discuss often. Begin today.

12. Surround Yourself With Healthy Foods. *Weigh yourself on accurate scales.* Weigh honestly and admit the truth to yourself. Weigh with a *weight loss goal* in mind.

Remember within you is the persistence and perseverance to win. Plan your daily diet on only those things that build your strength and energy.

13. Depression Rarely Occurs In Healthy Bodies. One doctor who has treated more people, more depression than any other doctor on earth has said, "I have never treated anyone with depression who was *physically* fit."

14. Good Habits Can Replace Bad Habits. God gave us one body. It is our responsibility to take care of it. We must! *One bad habit* can mess up your life. *One good habit* can turn your life around.

15. Find What Motivates You Toward Good Health. You must do all you can to regain the best quality of physical and mental health possible for you.

16. Small Changes Birth Great Rewards. It does not have to be radical changes...small ones done *consistently* will encourage you.

17. Develop An Obsession For *Water.* *Water is one of the best health habits to follow daily.* Keep a gallon jug or pitcher of water close by and drink throughout the day. Water literally "oils the machinery" of every organ of your body. Drink a minimum of 8 glasses of water daily.

18. Slow Down And Do Things The Right Way. Do *repeatedly* what you want to *increase* in your life. Remember...*Good health takes time.*

Good Health And Energy Is Necessary To Accomplish The Uncommon Dream God Has Given To

You.

The Uncommon Dream Will Require Good Health And Energy.

☙ 24 ☙

THE UNCOMMON DREAM IS SIMPLY YOUR HARVEST FROM UNCOMMON SEEDS

⎯⎯⎯►≡●≡◄⎯⎯⎯

God Wants You To Receive His Blessings.
The Bible reveals it. "No good thing will He withhold from them that walk uprightly," (Psalm 84:11). "Beloved, I wish above all things that thou mayest prosper and be in health, even as thy soul prospereth," (3 John 1:2).

You Can Give Your Way Out Of Trouble.
Open your heart and God will open His windows.

Everything You Have Comes From God. Everything you receive in the future will come from God. He is your total source for everything in life. *Never* forget this.

Jesus Taught That Giving Births The Beginning Of Blessings. "Give, and it shall be given unto you; good measure, pressed down, and shaken together and running over, shall men give into your bosom. For with the same measure that ye mete withal it shall be measured to you again," (Luke 6:38).

23 Facts About Your Seed

1. **A Seed Is Anything That Can Multiply And Become More.** Love is a Seed. Money is a Seed.

2. Everything You Possess Can Be Planted Back Into The World As A Seed. Think about the world as your soil and Seed bed to sow yourself into it!

3. Your Seed Is Anything That Benefits Another. Your forgiveness...kind words and time into others.

4. Your Harvest Is Anything That Benefits You. Favor from others. Your job and health!

5. Seed-Faith Simply Means To Plant Something You Have, Like A Seed, In Faith, For A Specific Harvest.

6. Your Seed Is A Photograph Of Your Faith. When you sow, you reveal your confidence in The Holy Spirit's potential result!

7. Seed-Faith Is Sowing Something You Have Been Given For (Toward) Something You Have Been Promised.

8. Your Seed Should Be Proportionate To The Harvest You Desire. How Big Is Your Uncommon Dream? What kind of Seed is necessary to plant to bring the Harvest you need? Seek The Holy Spirit. *He will bring to your mind what you already have.* When you sow love into your family, you will reap love. When you sow finances into the work of God, you will reap financial blessings.

9. The Secret Of Your Future Is Determined By The Seeds You Sow Today. You must sow into others lives. Remember Wisdom Key #6: *What You Make Happen For Others, God Will Make Happen For You.*

10. Your Tithe Is The Proof Of Your Trust. It is "The Tithe." *Never forget that ten percent of your income is Holy Seed.* "Bring ye all the tithes into the storehouse, that there may be meat in Mine house, and prove me now herewith, saith the Lord of hosts, if I will not open you the windows of heaven, and pour you out a blessing, that there shall not be room enough to receive it. And I will rebuke the devourer for your sakes, and he shall not destroy the fruits of your ground," (Malachi 3:10-11).

11. Your Seed Can Create Any Future You Want. Your Uncommon Dream will require that you participate in this principle. "Give and ye shall receive."

12. Everything You *Have* Is A Seed. What do you have that you can give? Who needs what you have to give? What do you need in exchange for your Seed? Who will profit from what you give?

God Had A Son But He Wanted A Family; He Sowed His Son To Create His Family. Millions are born again daily into the kingdom of *God because He gave His best Seed!*

13. Everything *Begins* With A Seed. Someone plants a small acorn. The acorn becomes a mighty oak tree. The small kernel of corn is planted. Each stalk produces two ears of corn. Each ear of corn contains over seven hundred kernels of corn. From that one small kernel of corn, a seed, 2,800 more kernels are created!

14. Whatever You Have Been Given Is Enough To Create Anything Else You Have Been Promised. You must discover that.

...The *sling* shot of David birthed his fame.

...The *rod* of Moses divided the Red Sea.

...The *meal* from the widow of Zarephath authorized Divine Provision throughout the famine (see 1 Kings 17).

15. Dependability Is The Seed For Promotion. If you sow the Seed of *diligence* on your job, the Harvest will be a *promotion*. "The soul of the sluggard desireth, and hath nothing: but the soul of the diligent shall be made fat," (Proverbs 13:4). "He becometh poor that dealeth with a slack hand: but the hand of the diligent maketh rich," (Proverbs 10:4).

16. Whatever You Are, You Will Create Around You. I am Irish. What will I create? *Irishmen.* What will a German create? *Germans.* What will a watermelon seed create? *Watermelons.* When you become generous with others, people around you desire to give to you. It is *simple, explosive and undeniable.*

17. Your Seed Is Guaranteed A 100-Fold Return. Jesus taught the 100-fold principle. "And Jesus answered and said, Verily I say unto you, There is no man that hath left house, or brethren, or sisters, or father, or mother, or wife, or children, or lands, for My sake, and the gospel's, But he shall receive an hundredfold now in this time, houses, and brethren, and sisters, and mothers, and children, and lands with persecutions; and in the world to come eternal life," (Mark 10:29-30).

18. Any Seed Of Nothing Will Create A Season Of Nothing. It is tragic beyond words if you fail to recognize your Seeds—what you have received from God to plant into the lives of others.

Stop focusing on losses. *Look longer, closer and thankfully at something you presently possess.*

19. Something You Already Have Is The Key To Your Future...*The Key To The Uncommon Dream.* *It may be knowledge, money, skills, or ideas,* *insights and concepts.*

20. If You Keep What You Have...That Is The Most It Will Ever Be. Releasing what you have is the only evidence of your faith that God will provide for you.

21. An Uncommon Seed Always Creates An Uncommon Harvest. An Uncommon Seed is one that requires Uncommon Faith...or a Seed you sow *during a season of Uncommon hardship.*

22. Recognition Of Your Seed Can Unlock A Thousand Harvests That Will Change Your Life Forever. What Seed can you sow that will make a difference in the urgency of your Dream? *What must happen to complete your Uncommon Dream?*

23. When You Sow What You Have Been Given, You Will Reap What You Have Been Promised.

As Dr. Oral Roberts told me at a quiet supper with me on his 80th birthday, "Mike, next to Jesus, the most sure thing on earth is that The Seed will multiply."

The Uncommon Dream Is Simply Your Harvest From Uncommon Seeds.

RECOMMENDED FOR YOUR WISDOM LIBRARY:

B-82 31 Reasons People Do Not Receive Their Financial Harvest (252 pages/$12)

The Price Of God's Presence
Is Simply Time.

-MIKE MURDOCK

≈ 25 ≈

THE UNCOMMON DREAM WILL CONTAIN SEASONS OF TESTING

Every Season Contains A Season Of Testing.
Everything in your life is a reward or a test.

Your Dream Is The Picture God Gave You To Keep You Motivated. Rewards are used to motivate the entire earth. God planned it that way. It is unnatural to pursue decrease. It is normal to pursue increase. This desire for gain is not satanic. Adam and Eve contained a desire for increase before they ever fell into sin. *The first command given to every living creature was to multiply.* You have the nature of God within you. The desire to grow is from Him.

13 Facts You Should Remember During A Season Of Testing

1. **The Holy Spirit Will Guide You Into A Time Of Testing.** "And Jesus being full of the Holy Ghost returned from Jordan, and was led by the Spirit into the wilderness, Being forty days tempted of the devil," (Luke 4:1-2).

You Must Qualify For The Uncommon Dream. The Holy Spirit will test you to qualify you for the promotion of The Uncommon Dream for which you have been striving. *The purpose of the testing is not mere survival.* It is to qualify you for the promotion...the increase of rewards.

2. The Uncommon Dream Is Always Tested By Unexpected Loss. *The desire for multiplication and increase is a characteristic of God.* "The thief cometh not, but for to steal, and to kill, and to destroy: I am come that they might have life, and that they might have it more abundantly," (John 10:10).

3. Loss Is Evidence Of An Expected Adversary, Loss Of Finances Or Job. The Holy Spirit led Jesus into the wilderness. He brought Him into a place of aloneness. Aloneness always concludes with a battle. *Every Uncommon Dream contains the test of aloneness.*

Remember Wisdom Key #246: *The Battle Of Your Life Is For Your Mind; The Battle Of The Mind Is For Focus.*

4. The Place Of Testing Is Always The Place Of Trust. The Holy Spirit will always carefully time your season of testing...*to qualify you for your season of reward.*

The Holy Spirit does not give you rewards for surviving your test. He provides you a test to qualify you for the rewards He desires you to experience.

5. Something You Can See Will Keep You Inspired For The Dream You Cannot See.

God keeps using everything He has made. He used the *stars* to motivate Abraham's faith for children.

Jesus used *water* to turn a marriage into a place of miracles when the wedding party ran out of wine.

Jesus used *clay and spittle* to unlock the faith of

a blind man.

Jesus used a *fish* to give Peter the money he needed for taxes.

The Holy Spirit uses *satan* to qualify you for a blessing. The Holy Spirit always brings you to a place of decision. He leads you to a place of testing.

6.   Every Question In Your Time Of Testing Has Been Pre-Answered In Scriptures. The Holy Spirit knows your tempter and the questions on the test and will provide every accurate answer necessary. The answers are always in The Word of God. *Always.*

7.   Your Knowledge Of Scriptures Decides Your Strength In Times Of Testing. When Jesus was being tempted, He did not cry out for special music so He could access the right frame of mind, or His most resourceful state.

He never said, "I must get back to the synagogue. I had no business coming out here alone." No, Jesus *knew* the answers.

As Jesus began to quote the eternal Word of God, satan became *demoralized* and *paralyzed*. *Jesus passed the test...the Anointing began to flow.*

8.   Expect   Your   Enemy   To   Make Unexpected Mistakes. Your enemy always makes mistakes. *Your only responsibility is to trust The Holy Spirit.*

The Holy Spirit never makes mistakes. Relax, in times of testing. Your Uncommon Dream is worth the testing. The Holy Spirit will not let you fail. He knows your enemy.

9.   Divine Words Demoralize Demonic Adversaries. You must keep His words in your mouth, your mind and in every conversation. His words are weapons. "For the weapons of our warfare are not carnal, but mighty through God to the pulling down of strongholds," (2 Corinthians 10:4).

10. The Holy Spirit Will Not Permit The Test To Be Too Great. "There hath no temptation taken you but such as is common to man: but God is faithful, who will not suffer you to be tempted above that ye are able; but will with the temptation also make a way to escape, that ye may be able to bear it," (1 Corinthians 10:13).

11. You Will Experience A Double Portion Of Influence And Provision As You Overcome Your Present Testing. It happened to Job. "And the Lord turned the captivity of Job, when he prayed for his friends: also the Lord gave Job twice as much as he had before," (Job 42:10).

12. Your Patience Births Great Disappointment To Your Enemies During Your Testing. That is why it is important for you to be patient, knowing that God will answer your prayers. "Behold, we count them happy which endure. Ye have heard of the patience of Job, and have seen the end of the Lord; that the Lord is very pitiful, and of tender mercy," (James 5:11). (See Chapter 22.)

13. Always Remember The Holy Spirit Will Decide The Timing Of Your Uncommon Dream. Thank Him for the season of testing. He has decided the *timing* and the *season of victory*.

Remember Wisdom Key #148: *The Holy Spirit Is The Only Person You Are Required To Obey.* He will also provide strength and empower you through every season. You will succeed and overcome. *Patiently praise Him as you enter into this wonderful season of promotion.*

> ▶ Your *Testing* Qualifies You For A Promotion.
> ▶ Your *Promotion* Qualifies You For Rewards.
> ▶ Your *Rewards* Will Increase The Flow Of Joy.

Expect *Testing* of Your Uncommon Dream.

The Holy Spirit Will Decide The Divine Timing Of The Uncommon Dream You Are Reaching For.

The Uncommon Dream Will Contain Seasons Of Testing.

When God Wants
   To Bless You
He Brings A Person
   Into Your Life.

-MIKE MURDOCK

∽ 26 ∽
THE UNCOMMON DREAM WILL REQUIRE BOTH DELEGATION AND NETWORKING WITH OTHERS

One Cannot Multiply.

You Can Succeed Significantly In Your Life.

You Can Have Incredible Relationships.

You Can Produce Finances Beyond Your Wildest Dreams.

However, you will never do it alone.

Life is a collection of relationships and those relationships compensate for what you do not have.

Imitate Your Master Mentor, Jesus.

Jesus *commanded* the multitudes.

He *instructed* His disciples to have the people sit down.

He *distributed* the loaves and fishes to His disciples for distribution.

Jesus gave instructions to a blind man to complete his healing. "When he had thus spoken, He spat on the ground, and made clay of the spittle, and He anointed the eyes of the blind man with the clay, And said unto him, Go, wash in the pool of Siloam, (which is by interpretation, Sent.) He went his way therefore, and washed, and came seeing," (John 9:6-7). Jesus sent His disciples into cities to prepare for special meals. (See Mark 14:12-15.)

7 Keys To Delegation And Networking

1. Acknowledge Your Own Limitations To Achieve Your Dream. When you do...*unexplainable energy ignites inside you.* Admitting your own limitations actually frees your mind to pursue the remedy and motivate others to assist you.

Remember Wisdom Key #102: *Anything You Do Not Have Is Stored In Someone Near You, And Love Is The Secret Map To The Treasure.* It is an internal integrity to admit your need for others.

2. Make A Checklist Of Their Specific Responsibilities. Avoid verbal instructions. Provide a written list of tasks to be accomplished.

3. Clarify Your Expectations Of Your Team. Confusion paralyzes. It neutralizes the flow of energy.

4. Provide Information And Authority Necessary To Complete Those Tasks. Inform others regarding the chain of authority. Identify openly who is authorized to instruct and who is expected to obey.

5. Establish Agreeable Deadlines To Complete The Tasks And Projects. Written plans unlock confidence in time lines and projected dates of completion.

6. Invest Time In Collaborative Conversation. This will bring others into harmony.

7. Remind Them Of Their Rewards For

Their Efforts. Always reward those who solve problems for you. Make the time to motivate and educate them as to your exact expectations. *Take the time to delegate. Jesus delegated.* Your Dream may require extraordinary negotiations.

The Secret Of Sam Walton

Sam Walton was a great negotiator. When he wanted to create the number one store in America, he went to his vendors. He negotiated with the owners of major companies for lower prices on their products. He told them his plan and said, "I will need your cooperation." He insisted, fought, and negotiated every inch of the way. He wanted to give his customers the best prices in America. He required the same from the manufacturers of his products.

Sam Walton knew the golden secrets necessary to make his own dreams come true. *He negotiated until he secured their cooperation.* Their companies received tremendous profits. You must nurture and protect those relationships connected to your Dream.

The Secret Of Dexter Yager

Dexter Yager is one of the most Uncommon men I know. I urge you to read his book, *Don't Let Anybody Steal Your Dream.* Dexter writes, *"The successful person associates with those who support his Dream."*

The Secret Of Solomon

Solomon knew you can never achieve a significant Dream without the involvement of people. He saw the hidden treasures in others around him in a way no one had seen before. He regarded the people around him as more than servants and employees. He saw them as more than sources of revenues and taxes.

His love was deep enough to ask God for uncommon ability to bless and strengthen those he governed. "Give therefore Thy servant an understanding heart to judge Thy people that I may discern between good and bad: for who is able to judge this Thy so great a people?" (1 Kings 3:9).

Love people enough *to empty your life into them.*

Love people enough *to pursue ways to reward them.*

Love people enough *to discern the dominant gift God has deposited in you for them.*

Within every human heart, beats a fervent desire to be needed, desired and celebrated. Recognize their differences and become their "bridge to greatness."

Solomon knew the principle and power of internal integrity. Denying his weakness would have paralyzed him. Now, he has an antenna, attracting *information, aid* and *encouragement* from others. You see, it is in the nature of man to help another. It is normal and natural...a trait God placed within us. When you try to do everything yourself, you prevent others from moving toward you. They feel *unnecessary, insignificant* and *unimportant* and you lose the *"gold mine"* placed within them.

The Uncommon Dream will always require the observation of others. Talk to those close to you. *Do not hesitate to ask them to tell you what they are seeing, hearing, and discovering.*

The Secret Of Steven K. Scott

As you pursue the dreams and goals for your life, take a sheet of paper and do what one of America's wealthiest men has suggested. Steven K. Scott, co-founder of the American Telecast Corporation, said in his book, *A Millionaire's Notebook*, *"List what you consider your greatest weakness,* both personally and professionally—lack of education, lack of career achievement, impatience, short temper, etc."

When you do this...you acknowledge your weaknesses and *attract those who are able to help you overcome them.*

Pursue The Secrets Of Others

Invest Time In Learning The Secret Of Others' Successes. Someone close to you contains answers.

Who has done what you want to do?

Who has had remarkable success?

Schedule appointments with them. Ask them to tell you what important questions you should ask.

Protocol Matters. Conduct yourself wisely in the presence of greatness. How you conduct yourself may determine whether you ever receive a second invitation. *Every Environment Requires A Code Of Conduct For Entering Or Remaining In It.*

The Uncommon Dream Will Require Adaptation To The Needs Of Those Around You. Never underestimate the importance of people. We live in a busy, hurried world. It is easy to be caught in the whirlwind of tasks and goals.

The Master Key to achieving The Uncommon Dream is inspiring those around you to become involved in its completion through network, collaboration and negotiation.

4 Qualities Of Wise Associations

1. **Those Who Speak Words That Increase Your Faith And Wisdom.** Become more selective in your friendships. Remember: The same time you waste on losers can be invested in winners.

2. **Those Who See The Worthiness Of Your God-Given Dream.** Listen for Wisdom around you. "If any of you lack wisdom, let him ask of God, that giveth to all men liberally, and upbraideth not; and it shall be given him," (James 1:5).

3. **Those Who Become Enthusiastic When You Enter Their Presence.** If you give time to those unworthy of it, *stop complaining.* You are the one who gave them the time. They abused it because you allowed them the opportunity.

4. **Those Who Remind You Of Your Special Gifts And Abilities.** Winners are people who have discovered their special talents, abilities, and special God-given gifts.

You can change the course of your life. A newcomer to town may fail to notice a traffic light and a collision results. Knowing the *"Stop and Go"* lights of life determine your tears or triumphs. Remember Wisdom Key #45: *The Willingness To Reach Births The Ability To Change.*

The Uncommon Dream Will Require Both Delegation And Networking With Others.

∾ 27 ∾
THE UNCOMMON DREAM WILL REQUIRE WISDOM IN SPECIFIC MATTERS

⟹▸◦◂⟸

Wisdom Is The Ability To Discern.

Discerning Right People And Wrong People. Good Decisions From Bad Decisions.

I love to see people succeed with their lives. It is also the desire of God, the Creator. As the artist treasures his painting, and the master craftsman the quality of the violin he created, so our Maker cherishes the *dreams, goals, excellence of life and the happiness you and I are to enjoy.*

Two Forces Are Vital To Happiness: *your relationships and your achievements or dreams.*

The Gospel Has Two Forces:

The Person of Jesus Christ and the Principles that He taught.

- ▶ One Is The **Son Of God;**
  The Other Is The **System Of God.**
- ▶ One Is The **Life Of God;**
  The Other Is The **Law Of God.**
- ▶ One Is **The King;**
  The Other Is **The Kingdom.**
- ▶ One Is **An Experience With God;**
  The Other Is **The Expertise Of God.**

▶ One Is **Heart-Related;**
The Other Is **Mind-Related.**

Salvation is experienced...*instantaneously.*
Principles are learned...*progressively.*

Both Forces Are Absolute Essentials To Total Success And Happiness.

It is important that you have a Dream or purpose in your life. Joseph dreamed a Dream.

Jesus had a purpose. Your dreams should be ordered of the Lord. "The steps of a good man are ordered by the Lord: and he delighteth in his way," (Psalm 37:23).

David wanted to build the temple, but his desire was not a God-intended goal. Solomon was the builder God had chosen.

Sometimes your personal desires are contradictory to God's plans. How do you know the difference? You find it in The Word, private prayer time and consultation with the Father.

You *discover* God's plans. *Usually, God's plans are revealed step-by-step.* If your Dream or desires persist, it probably is an indication that God wants you involved in that particular accomplishment. For example, God chose Solomon to build the temple, but David chose the materials.

You Must Know What God Wants You To Do Before You Can Do It. Be prepared by doing the following:

Look for Signs.
Listen to The Spirit.
Develop "Instant Response" to The Voice of God.
Eliminate the Time-Wasters in your life.

Concentrate on your God-Connections.

Understanding and Wisdom are the Golden Keys to mastering any situation in life.

The Word Of God Is The Wisdom Of God. "The entrance of Thy words giveth light; it giveth understanding unto the simple," (Psalm 119:130).

Wisdom Is Seeing What God Sees.

Wisdom Is The Golden Key To Achieving The Uncommon Dream. Knowledge is exploding all around us. Uncommon men of God are sharing their expertise and teaching us principles to change every area of our lives.

Your Uncommon Dream Will Require Uncommon Wisdom.

Two Sources Of Knowledge

1. **Mentors**—Learning From The Mistakes Of Others.

2. **Mistakes**—Learning From Your Own Mistakes.

If you are unhappy with yourself, dare to reach for new *information,* new *teaching* and new *truths* that will elevate you and build your relationship with God.

If there is a sin in your life, repent and rededicate your life to Jesus Christ. Allow His precious blood to cleanse you. He will restore the fellowship you need with Him.

12 Wisdom Principles That Will Bring You Closer To Your Uncommon Dream

1. **Never Speak Words That Make Satan**

Think He Is Winning. Your words are life. Express hope and confidence in God. Get so excited over planning your triumphs, you do not have time to complain over past losses.

2. **Life Changes Only When Your Daily Priorities Change.** Organize your time. Chart a detailed course with established deadlines. Set established time-sensitive goals. *When You Plan Your Day, You Have Planned Your Life.*

3. **Those Who Do Not Respect Your Time Will Not Respect Your Wisdom.** Cultivate discernment of people. Develop the ability to listen to God in the role someone has in your life.

4. **Stop Looking At What You See And Start Looking At What You Can Have.** Rebuild a good self-portrait. Sometimes we become more problem-oriented than possibility-oriented. Be thankful for the gifts God has given you. Concentrate on your strong points.

5. **Intolerance Of The Present Creates A Future.** Dare to embrace change. You are what you have decided to be. *Never Complain About What You Permit.*

6. **Whoever Cannot Increase You Will Eventually Decrease You.** Disconnect from unqualified persons who abuse and misuse your life. Re-evaluate your friendships. Do not allow your Dream to be destroyed because of someone who laughs at your pursuit of accomplishment.

7. **Your Words Are Signposts To Others— Pointing In The Direction Your Life Is Moving.** *Words are forces. Words are tools* God gave you to build your own spirit and mind. Control your mouth.

Your spirit and your body respond to words.

8. Any Disorder In Your Life Can Create The Death Of Your Dream. Millions of people who would not lie, cheat, or steal are immobilized by frustrations...*paralyzed* in their pursuit of spiritual goals. Be honest with yourself. Pinpoint the cause of your struggles. It could decide the life or death to your Dream.

9. Failure Will Last Only As Long As You Permit It. Realize that God is with you all the time. Depend on His presence to uphold you and keep you strong. You can become free when you "Practice" the presence of God.

10. Men Do Not Really Decide Their Future...They Decide Their Habits—Then, Their Habits Decide Their Future. Control the circumstances within your power. Decide what you can change. Start developing habits that will affect your future Dreams and goals.

11. You Will Never Leave Where You Are Until You Decide Where You Would Rather Be. It is normal to experience a few setbacks, moments of doubt and confusion. Make this your confession. "I can do all things through Christ which strengtheneth me," (Philippians 4:13).

12. The Seasons Of Your Life Will Change Every Time You Decide To Use Your Faith. Remember...

God made you to soar...*not sink!*
God made you to fly...*not fall!*
God made you to stand...*not stumble!*

▶ Keep A Wisdom Journal.
▶ Cultivate Ease At Dictating Your

Thoughts Into A Digital Recorder.
► Make Your Mind A Constant
Interrogater Of Your Environment.
► Create Your Information System,
Computer And Scanner.

The Uncommon Dream Will Require Wisdom In Specific Matters.

≈ 28 ≈
THE UNCOMMON DREAM WILL REQUIRE MIND-MANAGEMENT

Your Mind Is Your World.

What Happens In Your Mind Will Happen In Time. Never justify failure. Refuse to bog down in placing blame on others. Reach up for the key out of your difficulties.

Happiness Begins In Your Mind. Your mind is the drawing room for tomorrow's circumstances.

Mind-Management Is The Key To Success... Energy. "Whatsoever things are true, whatsoever things are honest, whatsoever things are just, whatsoever things are pure, whatsoever things are lovely, whatsoever things are of good report; if there be any virtue, and if there be any praise, think on these things," (Philippians 4:8).

Winners Are Simply Ex-Losers That Got Mad. They were tired of failure. The day you get angry at your failures is the day you start winning.

Winning does not start around you—it begins inside your MIND. Winning attracts opposition.

Adversity Has Advantages.

▶ It Reveals The Depth Of Friendships.

▶ It Will Force You To Search For More

Accurate Information.

▶ It Will Help You Decide What You Really Believe.

14 Power Keys For Managing Your Mind

1. Discern The True Definition Of Success. Success is the progressive achievement of a God-given goal.

2. Set Definite Goals For Yourself. You do not merely set your goals, but set them under divine guidance.

3. Make Your Goals Balanced And Reasonable. Over-emphasis in one area will cause another area to deteriorate. "The wisdom of the prudent is to understand his way," (Proverbs 14:8).

4. Meditate In Scripture. The mentality of God is absorbed through simply reading The Word of God. It gives you discerning ability for what is false and what is true.

5. Discern The Spiritual Mentor That Most Increases Your Confidence In The Word Of God. Invest time in finding the right church and then be loyal. Attend consistently. Volunteer your time as a Seed and God will honor you greatly.

6. Schedule Time With Uncommon Achievers. Be a learner. "He that walketh with wise men shall be wise," (Proverbs 13:20).

7. Invest In Yourself. Develop your *mind*, *spirit* and *inner* man. If a $20 meal makes your stomach feel good for four hours, think what it could do to your mentality and power-life to invest $20 in tapes or books that soak your mind and spirit in the anointing of God.

8. Stay Steadily Productive And In Movement. Time-wasters grieve God. Idleness results in *frustration, boredom* and possibly even *depression*.

9. Identify Your Dominant Distinction From Others And Build Your Thought Life Around It. Take a good look at yourself. You are accountable to God for developing your skills. *Everyone's talents and gifts differ.*

Though a man is compensated by other men according to their need for his special gifts, God values every man's abilities and gifts equally. You must do the same. *Value the greatness of your gifts.* Invest time to improve them. The special talents God has given to you will generate everything you will need to be financially successful, but *you must grow the Seeds within you.*

10. You Must Cultivate A Teachable Spirit. Willingness to change is not necessarily a compromise of principles.

11. Unwrap Your Present Moments And Savor The Divine Difference You Discern In Them. Every moment you want to feel in your future is already in your present. It took you a lifetime to get to this moment...*why are you racing from it?*

12. Remind Yourself That Something God Has Hidden Within You Is Keeping Him Very Interested In His Investment. You feel like an acorn. God is looking at the oak tree you are becoming. Remember Wisdom Key #275: *The Greatest Success Quality On Earth Is The Willingness To Become.*

13. Sowing The Seed Of Adaptation Is Proof Of Genius. *Flexibility* and *openness* to truth are evidence you are a winner. Sometimes it takes courage to listen. Time and knowledge should enlarge you. Let it change you. Do not be a "know it all." Remember Wisdom Key # 268: *The First Step Toward Success Is The Willingness To Listen.*

14. Use Your Mouth To Master Your Mind. *You become what you think.*

Picture Yourself In Health.

Picture Yourself In Prosperity.

Picture Yourself In A Happy Marriage.

Picture Yourself As An Overcomer.

Picture Yourself As Victorious.

When you control your thoughts, you control your life. "Whatsoever things are true...honest...just... pure...lovely...of good report; if there be any virtue, if there be any praise, think on these things," (Philippians 4:8). Visualize what you want to materialize.

You Are Well On Your Way To Accomplishing Your Uncommon Dream When You Develop Mind-Management.

The Uncommon Dream Will Require Mind-Management.

❧ 29 ❧

THE UNCOMMON DREAM WILL REQUIRE CONTINUOUS OBEDIENCE

Obedience Is Completing An Instruction.
Obedience Is The Only Thing God Has Ever Required Of Man. "If ye love Me, keep My commandments. And I will pray the Father, and He shall give you another Comforter, that He may abide with you for ever," (John 14:15-16).

15 Power Thoughts On Obedience

1. Your Obedience Always Brings Pleasure To God. "Learn to do well; seek judgment, relieve the oppressed, judge the fatherless, plead for the widow. Come now, and let us reason together, saith the Lord: though your sins be as scarlet, they shall be as white as snow; though they be red like crimson, they shall be as wool," (Isaiah 1:17-18).

2. The Obedient Are Promised Prosperity. "If ye be willing and obedient, ye shall eat the good of the land: But if ye refuse and rebel, ye shall be devoured with the sword: for the mouth of the Lord hath spoken it," (Isaiah 1:19-20).

3. The Obedient Are The Only Ones Who Qualify For Blessings. "But He said, Yea, rather, blessed are they that hear the word of God, and keep it," (Luke 11:28).

4. The Obedient Are Guaranteed Safety. *Obedience to The Word guarantees your personal safety.* "Wherefore ye shall do My statutes, and keep My judgments, and do them; and ye shall dwell in the land in safety," (Leviticus 25:18).

5. The Obedient Affects The Destiny Of Many Generations In Their Own Families. "And in thy seed shall all the nations of the earth be blessed; because thou hast obeyed My voice," (Genesis 22:18).

6. The Obedient Document Their Trust In God. *Obedience is the only proof of your faith in God.* You asked God for a miracle. He gives you an instruction. When you obey the instruction, it is proof that you believe what He said.

7. The Obedient Learn What Others Never Do. "Though He were a Son, yet learned He obedience by the things which He suffered; And being made perfect, He became the author of eternal salvation unto all them that obey Him," (Hebrews 5:8-9).

8. The Obedient Qualify For A Personal Relationship With God. Obedience creates your relationship with God. "And He answered and said unto them, My mother and My brethren are these which hear the word of God, and do it," (Luke 8:21).

As Christians, we need to *implement, embrace* and *build* on the knowledge of properly following instructions.

Ask The Holy Spirit to wake up a desire in you to follow His instructions. He desires obedience from His children above all.

Obedience always creates waves of blessing.

Obedience To The Counsel Of Your Spiritual Mentor. To follow your Uncommon Dream...there will be times that you will receive instructions from someone in an advisory position. It could be your pastor or a mentor you have chosen to lead you.

Simple obedience will be the path to pursue. Even when you do not understand something...you have to trust. Their decisions are not always logical but on a supernatural revelation from God.

I can trace most of the pain in my life to an ignored instruction...*an act of disobedience.*

You cannot build a *future*...a *vision*...an *Uncommon Dream* if there is not enough respect to follow someone's instructions.

9. Your Reaction To A Man Of God Determines God's Reaction To You.

Your reaction to His authority is your way of *honoring* or *dishonoring* Him. *What are you doing with the instructions God has already given you?* What are you doing with the instructions of your supervisor?

10. You Can Only Be Promoted By Someone Whose Instructions You Have Followed. Follow the instructions of the authority over you. Also, expect your employees to follow your instructions.

Ask The Holy Spirit to give you understanding about how *obedience* produces *rewards.* Remember Wisdom Key #14: *The Instruction You Follow Determines The Future You Create.*

11. Obedience Produces Victories. Achan was a man in the Bible who *did not follow* an instruction and there was weeping in every tent in

Israel because of his disobedience.

12. God Will Never Advance You Beyond Your Last Act Of Disobedience.

13. Obedience May Create A Temporary Season Of Loss. Obedience is rarely easy. Some losses are unavoidable. However, those losses are necessary and essential for long-term gains.

God has reasons for every demand He makes on your life. You must see *Treasures beyond your Losses.*

The Double Portion Blessing Of God Can Follow Every Major Loss. It happened when Job lost his children, his flocks and herds, and his position of credibility and popularity. "And the Lord turned the captivity of Job, when he prayed for his friends: also the Lord gave Job twice as much as he had before," (Job 42:10-12).

14. There Is No More Disrespect That Can Be Shown Than To Ignore Or Refuse To Follow An Instruction Given. You are never responsible for the pain of those who ignore your counsel.

15. Obedience Increases Your Worth.

When a dog is obedient, its worth soars. There are schools of obedience for dogs that are very costly. It also increases the price of the dog.

Many animals learn obedience for circus routines to perform at zoos. Men make fortunes from obedient animals.

10 Master Keys To Following Instructions

1. Never Treat An Instruction Lightly.

▶ *An instruction should be clear, precise and understandable.*

▶ *Instructions move any project toward completion.*

▶ *Instructions are to lighten the load.*

▶ *Instructions are explicit to avoid waste of money.*

2. Instructions Must Come From The One Authorized And Qualified To Give It.

▶ *Must be thorough and complete...*

▶ *Must be spoken clearly...*

▶ *Must be understood...*

▶ *Must be given to the one responsible for its completion...*

▶ *Must have time definition...*

3. Listen To The Instruction Completely.

▶ *Listen to details...*

▶ *Schedules expected...*

▶ *Problems anticipated...*

▶ *Color...Size...*

▶ *Qualities...Quantities...*

▶ *Note what was not said so you can ask appropriate questions.*

4. Repeat Back The Instructions.

▶ *The person giving the instruction...needs to hear exactly what you heard.*

▶ *Sometimes something was thought but...not really spoken.*

▶ *The employee sometimes hears only a part of an instruction.*

▶ *Sometimes both assume the other knows what they are thinking and discussing.*

▶ *Say it back clearly...completely.*

5. Complete The Instruction.

▶ *Do it the way it was expected.*

▶ *Do it completely and thoroughly.*

▶ *Report any problems you may encounter.*

6. Report To The Person Who Gave You The Instruction.

▶ *Report progress and status as it continues.*

▶ *Report it continuously.*

▶ *Report it back honestly.*

When an instruction is ignored—the very opposite has occurred. *Any ignored instruction will create a loss of time energy or money.*

7. Never Trivialize An Instruction.

▶ Do not play it down. "I know pastor said he wanted that, but you know sometimes he changes his mind."

▶ Disrespect is evident by unkind remarks.

8. Prevent "Forgotten Instructions."

▶ Write it down. A short pencil is longer than a long memory.

▶ Use a Day Timer to keep track of instructions and important information.

▶ Use your mind for creativity not memory.

9. Do Not Alter Instructions.

▶ Gain an understanding of what is being said and then write it down.

▶ Then repeat back to your instructor what you understood them to say.

10. Do Not Neglect An Instruction.

▶ Do not challenge an instruction. If you have something to say about it...call your leader aside and clarify or ask for more information.

The Uncommon Dream Will Require Continuous Obedience.

Submission Cannot Begin
Until Agreement Ends.

-MIKE MURDOCK

❧ 30 ❧

THE UNCOMMON DREAM WILL REQUIRE SUBMISSION TO SOMEONE

Authority Is Not Permission To Dominate.

Authority is permission to protect. The purpose of authority is not merely to restrict, but rather to advance another, to recognize and reward their obedience. Authority requires qualification.

3 Rewards For Submitting To Legitimate Authority

Those Who Rule Over You Are Instructed To Reward You. "Withhold not good from them to whom it is due, when it is in thine hand to do it," (Proverbs 3:27).

1. Qualified Authority Should Offer Protection To You. Note that God did not simply instruct you to bring the tithe to Him. He promised to protect everything you create and generate.

The covenant rewards everyone involved.

2. Qualified Authority Should Produce Provision For You. That is exactly what God promises you. "If thou shalt hearken diligently unto the voice of the Lord thy God, to observe and to do all His commandments which I command thee this day, that the Lord thy God will set thee on high above all nations of the earth," (Deuteronomy 28:1).

3. Qualified Authority Should Promote You. The true source of promotion comes from God. "For promotion cometh neither from the east, nor from the west, nor from the south. But God is the judge: He putteth down one, and setteth up another," (Psalm 75:6-7).

16 Facts You Should Know About Submission

1. Your Submission Is The Willingness To Embrace The Leadership Of Those Responsible For Governing Your Life. Submission is rewarded when it is followed according to The Word of God. There will be many different seasons in discovering your Dream.

2. Your Submission Is A Personal Choice. "God resisteth the proud, but giveth grace unto the humble. Humble yourselves in the sight of the Lord and He shall lift you up," (James 4:6, 10).

3. Your Submission Reveals Humility. Some people assume that leadership is strength and submission implies weakness. However, true submission is evidence of flexibility, trust and humility. It is the quality of champions. Humility is the gate to promotion.

4. Your Submission Is Your Personal Gift Of Cooperation To Those Who Govern You. Every great leader began as a great follower. They honored authority established by God. "Obey them that have rule over you, and submit yourselves: for they watch for your souls, as they that must give account, that they may do it with joy, and not with grief: for that is unprofitable for you," (Hebrews 13:17).

5. Your Submission To Authority Reflects The Nature Of Jesus Within You. When Jesus prayed in the Garden of Gethsemane, He prayed this prayer before Calvary. "O My Father, if it be possible, let this cup pass from Me: nevertheless not as I will, but as Thou wilt," (Matthew 26:39).

6. Your Submission Should Eventually Result In Inner Joy. "Looking unto Jesus the Author and Finisher of our faith; Who for the joy that was set before Him endured the cross, despising the shame, and is set down at the right hand of the throne of God," (Hebrews 12:2).

7. Your Submission To A Mentor Qualifies You For His Anointing. Elisha received a double portion of Elijah's anointing as a reward.

8. Your Refusal To Submit To The Chain Of Authority Will Schedule Seasons Of Tragedy. "But if ye refuse and rebel, ye shall be devoured with the sword: for the mouth of the Lord hath spoken it," (Isaiah 1:20).

9. Your Submission To A True Man-Woman Of God Will Produce Prosperity. "Believe in the Lord your God, so shall ye be established; believe His prophets, so shall ye prosper," (2 Chronicles 20:20).

10. Your Submission To A Wise And Qualified Spiritual Leadership Is A Scriptural Command. "Remember them which have the rule over you, who have spoken unto you the Word of God: whose faith follow, considering the end of their conversation," (Hebrews 13:7).

11. Your Submission In Honoring And Respecting Others Reveals Your Fear Of God. "Submitting yourselves one to another in the fear of God," (Ephesians 5:21). "Whosoever therefore shall humble himself as this little child, the same is greatest in the kingdom of heaven," (Matthew 18:4).

12. Your Submission Reveals The Fear Of God And Guarantees Supernatural Provision And Promotion. "By humility and the fear of the Lord are riches, and honor, and life," (Proverbs 22:4).

13. Your Submission To Authority Is Often Reproduced In Those Who Serve You. *What you are, you will create around you.* When you submit to those over you, it motivates those under your rule to submit to you as well. You become their example. *Those who govern you are also under the authority of God.*

14. Your Submission To The Word Of God Will Unleash Uncommon Wisdom Within You. The Scriptures are able, "...to make thee wise unto salvation through faith which is in Christ Jesus...That the man of God may be perfect, throughly furnished unto all good works," (2 Timothy 3:15-17).

15. Your Submission Is A Seed That Eventually Results In The Harvest Of Honor. Do not be weary, when you feel stressed, overwhelmed and incapable of meeting the requirements of others. "And let us not be weary in well doing: for in due season ye shall reap, if we faint not," (Galatians 6:9).

16. Your Submission Is The Divine Link To A Person Who Observes, Respects And Elevates You Into Your Uncommon Dream. God often uses someone in authority over you to advance your Assignment to help discover your Uncommon Dream.

▶ Ruth *submitted* to Naomi who linked her to Boaz.

▶ Naaman *submitted* to the prophet and his leprosy disappeared.

▶ The widow of Zeraphath *submitted* to The Seed instruction of Elijah and reaped a Harvest in the midst of famine.

The Uncommon Dream Will Require Submission To Someone.

Warfare Always Surrounds The Birth Of A Miracle.

-MIKE MURDOCK

∾ 31 ∾
THE UNCOMMON DREAM WILL REQUIRE THE HEART OF A WARRIOR

━━━━━━━▰◦◦◦◦▰━━━━━━━

Warfare Is Inevitable.

Your Enemy Observes All Progress.

The Holy Spirit is your Mentor for seasons of battle and warfare, "He teacheth my hands to war, so that a bow of steel is broken by mine arms," (Psalm 18:34). "Blessed be the Lord my strength, which teacheth my hands to war, and my fingers to fight," (Psalm 144:1).

Completion of your *Assignment* will cause the completion of your *Dream.* It will also require the *Nature, Skills and Mentality of a Warrior.*

18 Qualities Of The Uncommon Warrior

1. The Uncommon Warrior Only Uses The Weapons That Have Never Failed Him. David refused to use the weapons. David used the weapon he was most familiar with—his sling. (See 1 Samuel 17:38-40.)

2. The Uncommon Warrior Refuses To Use The Armor And Weaponry Of Others Who Had Failed Before Him. David did. "And Saul armed David with his armor, and he put an helmet of brass upon his head: also he armed him with a coat of mail. And David girded his sword upon his armor, and he assayed to go; for he had not proved it. And David said unto Saul, I cannot go with these; for I have not proved them. And David put them off him," (1 Samuel 17:38-39).

3.   **The Uncommon Warrior Knows He Has Something His Enemy Should Fear.** David had a willingness to fight. "And David said to Saul, Let not man's heart fail because of him; thy servant will go and fight with this Philistine," (1 Samuel 17:32).

4.   **The Uncommon Warrior Knows The True Source Of His Competence And Confidence.** David did. "David said moreover, The Lord that delivered me out of the paw of the lion, and out of the paw of the bear, He will deliver me out of the hand of this Philistine," (1 Samuel 17:37).

5.   **The Uncommon Warrior Knows That The Power Of God Is Greater Than The Weapons Of Man.** David did. "Then said David to the Philistine, Thou comest to me with a sword, and with a spear and with a shield: but I come to thee in the name of the Lord of hosts, the God of the armies of Israel, whom thou hast defied," (1 Samuel 17:45).

6.   **The Uncommon Warrior Often Uses, In His Greatest Battle, The Skills Developed In His Daily Routine.** David did. He was accustomed to protecting the sheep of his father. "And he took his staff in his hand, and chose him five smooth stones out of the brook, and put them in a shepherd's bag which he had, even in a scrip; and his sling was in his hand: and he drew near to the Philistine," (1 Samuel 17:40).

7.   **The Uncommon Warrior Expects To Be**

An Instrument In The Hand Of God To Destroy His Enemy. David did. He said, "And I will smite thee, and take thine head from thee; and I will give the carcases of the host of the Philistines this day unto the fowls of the air, and to the wild beasts of the earth; that all the earth may know that there is a God in Israel," (1 Samuel 17:46).

8. The Uncommon Warrior Expects His Enemies To Fall And He Publicly Predicts His Victory. David did. "This day will the Lord deliver thee into mine hand," (1 Samuel 17:46). "When mine enemies are turned back, they shall fall and perish at Thy presence," (Psalm 9:3).

9. The Uncommon Warrior Stays On The Offensive Running Toward His Enemies. David did. "And it came to pass, when the Philistine arose, and came and drew nigh to meet David, that David hasted, and ran toward the army to meet the Philistine," (1 Samuel 17:48).

10. The Uncommon Warrior Expects The Spectators Of The Battle To Observe And Experience The Power Of God. David did. "And all this assembly shall know that the Lord saveth not with sword and spear: for the battle is the Lord's, and He will give you into our hands," (1 Samuel 17:47).

11. The Uncommon Warrior Keeps Vibrant Memories Of Past Victories. David did. "And David said unto Saul, Thy servant kept his father's sheep, and there came a lion, and a bear, and took a lamb out of the flock: And I went out after him, and smote him, and delivered it out of his mouth: and when he arose against me, I caught him by his beard, and smote him, and slew him. Thy servant slew both the lion and the bear: and this uncircumcised Philistine shall be as one of them, seeing he hath defied the armies of the living God," (1 Samuel 17:34-36).

12. The Uncommon Warrior Ignores The Opinions Of Obvious Losers And Failures Around Him. David did. "And Eliab his eldest brother heard when he spake unto the men; and Eliab's anger was kindled against David, and he said, Why camest thou down hither? and with whom hast thou left those few sheep in the wilderness? I know thy pride, and the naughtiness of thine heart; for thou art come down that thou mightest see the battle. And David said, What have I now done? Is there not a cause? And he turned from him toward another, and spake after the same manner: and the people answered him again after the former manner," (1 Samuel 17:28-30).

13. The Uncommon Warrior Pursues, Savors And Celebrates The Rewards Of Every Victory. David did. "And the men of Israel said, Have ye seen this man that is come up? surely to defy Israel is he come up: and it shall be, that the man who killeth him, the king will enrich him with great riches, and will give him his daughter, and make his father's house free in Israel. And David spake to the men that stood by him, saying, What shall be done to the man that killeth this Philistine, and taketh away the reproach from Israel? for who is this uncircumcised Philistine, that he should defy the armies of the living God?" (1 Samuel 17:25-26).

14. The Uncommon Warrior Keeps His Promise To Destroy His Enemy. David did.

"Therefore David ran, and stood upon the Philistine, and took his sword, and drew it out of the sheath thereof, and slew him, and cut off his head therewith," (1 Samuel 17:51).

15. The Uncommon Warrior Unashamedly Displays The Spoils Of Past Victories As Trophies Of Thanksgiving. David did. David even carried the head of Goliath around with him. "And as David returned from the slaughter of the Philistine, Abner took him, and brought him before Saul with the head of the Philistine in his hand," (1 Samuel 17:57).

16. The Uncommon Warrior Creates His Own Museum Of Memories To Celebrate His Victories. David did. "And David took the head of the Philistine, and brought it to Jerusalem; but he put his armor in his tent," (1 Samuel 17:54).

17. The Uncommon Warrior Knows That The Defeat Of His Strongest Adversary Will Cause His Other Enemies To Flee. David saw this. When Goliath fell, his followers fled. "And when the Philistines saw their champion was dead, they fled," (1 Samuel 17:51).

18. The Uncommon Warrior Knows That When He Is Victorious, The Discouraged Around Him Become Encouraged And Energized. David saw this happen. "And the men of Israel and Judah arose, and shouted, and pursued the Philistines, until thou come unto the valley, and to the gates of Ekron. And the wounded of the Philistines fell down by the way to Shaaraim, even unto Gath, and unto Ekron," (1 Samuel 17:52).

The Uncommon Dream Will Require The Heart Of A Warrior.

My Prayer For You,

"Holy Spirit, I am an overcomer. Like David, I am willing to confront my adversary, defeat him and unleash the aroma of victory in my world, my job, my home and to those to whom I am assigned.

Impart into me today the renewed zeal of a Spirit Warrior...destroying the strongholds of satan and setting captives free.

I am your *Deliverer* on the earth, anointed to drive back the darkness with the Wisdom of God. Pour the healing oil of Calvary on the wounds of the broken.

I will fight and win...my battle for the Uncommon Dream. In the name of Jesus, Amen."

WISDOM KEYS TO REMEMBER

The Battle Of Your Life Is For Your Mind: The Battle Of The Mind Is For Focus. (Wisdom Key #246)

When Satan Wants To Destroy You He Puts A Person In Your Life. (Wisdom Key #215)

An Uncontested Enemy Will Flourish. (Wisdom Key #117)

Your Significance Is Not In Your Similarity To Another; But In Your Point Of Difference From Another. (Wisdom Key #54)

When You Let Go Of What Is In Your Hand, God Will Let Go Of What Is In His Hand. (Wisdom Key #4)

The Pursuit Of The Mentor Reveals The Passion Of The Protegé. (Wisdom Key #297)

Every Friendship Nurtures A Strength Or A Weakness. (Wisdom Key #123)

Champions Make Decisions That Create The Future They Desire; Losers Make Decisions That Create The Present They Desire. (Wisdom Key #343)

If You Do Not Know Where You Belong, You Will Adapt

To Where You Are. (Wisdom Key #129)

What You Make Happen For Others, God Will Make Happen For You. (Wisdom Key #6)

The Holy Spirit Is The Only Person You Are Required To Obey. (Wisdom Key #148)

Anything You Do Not Have Is Stored In Someone Near You, And Love Is The Secret Map To The Treasure. (Wisdom Key #102)

The Willingness To Reach Births The Ability To Change. (Wisdom Key #45)

The Greatest Success Quality On Earth Is The Willingness To Become. (Wisdom Key #275)

The First Step Toward Success Is The Willingness To Listen. (Wisdom Key #268)

The Instruction You Follow Determines The Future You Create. (Wisdom Key #14)

31 DAYS TO ACHIEVING YOUR DREAM

1. Your Dream Is Anything You Want To *Become*, *Do* Or *Have* During Your Lifetime.
2. Your Dream Must Be *Believed*, *Pursued* And *Protected* To Be Achieved.
3. Your Dream Can Come True Regardless Of Your Personal Limitations.
4. Your Dream Should Always Determine What You Do *First* Each Morning.
5. The Dream You Are Pursuing Will Always Control And Dictate Your Daily Conduct And Behavior.
6. Your Daily Conversation Is A Portrait Of Your Passion For The Dream You Are Pursuing.
7. Every Daily *Appointment* Should Be A Stepping Stone Toward The Fulfillment Of Your Dream.
8. Your Dream May Birth Changes In Your Relationships.
9. Your Dream Will Determine Who Reaches For You.
10. Your Dream Should Be Born Within You, Not Borrowed From Others.
11. Your Dream May Require A Geographical Change.
12. Your Dream Determines Who Qualifies For Access.
13. Your Dream Should Qualify For Your Total Focus.
14. Your Dream Will Require Seasons Of Preparation.
15. Achieving Your Dream May Require An Uncommon Mentor.
16. Your Dream Is Your True Significant Difference From Another.
17. Satan Will Often Use Memories Of Your Past Failures To Distort The Dream God Is Developing

In You.

18. Your Success Cannot Begin Until You Fuel Your Passion For The Dream Within You.

19. Your Family May Often Focus On Your Weaknesses Instead Of The Dream Growing Within You.

20. If You Neglect The Dream Within You, It Will Eventually Wither And Die.

21. Your Dream May Require Uncommon Faith.

22. Your Dream May Be Birthed From Uncommon Tragedies And Painful Memories.

23. Your Dream May Be Misunderstood By Those Closest To You.

24. Your Dream May Be So Great That It Makes You Feel Fearful, Inadequate Or Inferior.

25. Your Dream Is Your Invisible Companion Accompanying You From Your Present Into Your Future.

26. The Passion For Your Dream Must Increase So Strong That It Burns Within You Without The Encouragement Of Others.

27. Your Dream May Expose Adversarial Relationships In Your Life.

28. Your Dream Will Require Uncommon Favor From Others.

29. Every Relationship Will Move You Toward Your Dream Or Away From It.

30. When You Boldly Announce Your Dream, You Will Create An Instant Bond With Every Person Who Wants To Accomplish The Same Dream.

31. You Must Practice Continual Visualization Of Your Dream.

DECISION

Will You Accept Jesus As Your Personal Savior Today?

The Bible says, "That if thou shalt confess with thy mouth the Lord Jesus, and shalt believe in thine heart that God hath raised Him from the dead, thou shalt be saved," (Romans 10:9).

Pray this prayer from your heart today!

"Dear Jesus, I believe that You died for me and rose again on the third day. I confess I am a sinner...I need Your love and forgiveness...Come into my heart. Forgive my sins. I receive Your eternal life. Confirm Your love by giving me peace, joy and supernatural love for others. Amen."

DR. MIKE MURDOCK

is in tremendous demand as one of the most dynamic speakers in America today.

More than 16,000 audiences in 39 countries have attended his Schools of Wisdom and conferences. Hundreds of invitations come to him from churches, colleges and business corporations. He is a noted author of over 200 books, including the best sellers, *The Leadership Secrets of Jesus* and *Secrets of the Richest Man Who Ever Lived*. Thousands view his weekly television program, *Wisdom Keys with Mike Murdock*. Many attend his Schools of Wisdom that he hosts in many cities of America.

Clip and Mail

☐ Yes, Mike! I made a decision to accept Christ as my personal Savior today. Please send me my free gift of your book, *31 Keys to a New Beginning* to help me with my new life in Christ.

NAME   BIRTHDAY

ADDRESS

CITY   STATE   ZIP

PHONE   E-MAIL

Mail form to: **The Wisdom Center** · 4051 Denton Hwy.
Ft. Worth, TX 76117 · 1-817-759-BOOK · 1-817-759-0300
You Will Love Our Website...! www.TheWisdomCenter.tv

Wisdom Key 3000

TODAY!

Will You Become My Ministry Partner In The Work Of God?

Dear Friend,

God has connected us!

I have asked The Holy Spirit for 3000 Special Partners who will plant a monthly Seed of $58.00 to help me bring the gospel around the world. (58 represents 58 kinds of blessings in the Bible.)

Will you become my monthly Faith Partner in The Wisdom Key 3000? Your monthly Seed of $58.00 is so powerful in helping heal broken lives. When you sow into the work of God, 4 Miracle Harvests are guaranteed in Scripture, Isaiah 58...

▶ Uncommon Health (Isaiah 58)

▶ Uncommon Wisdom For Decision-Making (Isaiah 58)

▶ Uncommon Financial Favor (Isaiah 58)

▶ Uncommon Family Restoration (Isaiah 58)

Your Faith Partner,

Mike Murdock

P.S. Please clip the coupon attached and return it to me today, so I can rush the Wisdom Key Partnership Pak to you...or call me at 1-817-759-0300.

PP-03

☐ *Yes Mike, I want to join The Wisdom Key 3000.*
  Please rush The Wisdom Key Partnership Pak to me today!
☐ *Enclosed is my first monthly Seed-Faith Promise of:*
  ☐ *$58* ☐ *Other $_____.*

☐ CHECK ☐ MONEY ORDER ☐ AMEX ☐ DISCOVER ☐ MASTERCARD ☐ VISA

Credit Card # _____ Exp. ____/____

Signature _____

Name _____ Birth Date ____/____/____

Address _____

City _____ State _____ Zip _____

Phone _____ E-Mail _____

THE WISDOM CENTER 1-817-759-BOOK
4051 Denton Highway • Fort Worth, TX 76117 1-817-759-0300

You Will Love Our Website:
www.TheWisdomCenter.tv

It Could Happen

Unexpected Insurance Check...!

I will share the miracles and blessings of the $58 Seed that I wrapped my faith around this month. The insurance company told me the other insurance company did not want to pay the first $500 that I had put out when we were hit. Well this month a restoration check for $500 arrived in the mail.

N. G. - Whiting, NJ

Electric Bill Paid...!

I just wanted to write and thank you for your prayers and to let you know that we have experienced miracles from God. My daughter and son-in-law were behind by $1,000 on their electric bill. They were later informed that their bill had been paid in full. My son had to go to the hospital with no medical insurance. He received a bill for $3,800. A few days later he got another statement with the amount owed marked $0. It had been paid by a charitable organization that operates within the hospital. I'm happy to have made the $58 month pledge and to be one your Wisdom Key 3000 faith partners.

J. & S. H. - Tunnel Hill, IL

Custody Battle Solved...!

We sent in a $58 Seed for half, if not full custody of my husband's children from a previous marriage. We received half custody. Also, $68,000 of child support which was owed was erased.

M. & A. M. - Seattle, WA

Healing...!

My praise report is that I gave a $58 Seed and my health has been improving in my body. I asked you to pray for my lymphatic system and muscles that had broken down and shut down. Every day I feel strength in my legs I haven't felt before and I can tell the difference in my walk, and I am losing weight. I feel my strength coming back.

C. G. - Lynchburg, VA

Financial Blessing...!

I am 91 years old. I conduct a weekly prayer teaching fellowship at the senior facility where I live. I am so blessed by how God is using you. I can testify to sowing a $58 Seed and receiving $2,000. I was then able to pay the pledge in full for the entire remaining $58 Seeds.

M. G. - Muskegon, MI

A New Car...!

I do have a praise report. My last $58 Seed was for a new truck. Well, I'm driving a new Lincoln Navigator. Also I received 2 new students already for my school.

C. D. - Minnetonka, MN

Unexpected Check...!

Several months ago I was watching your program on TV and I felt I was one who should plant a $58 Seed. On the very day I received written acknowledgement of that Seed, I also received in the mail a very unexpected check for more than $1,400. It was sorely needed at the time.

R. D. - St. Louis, MO

It Could Happen To You!

Tax Reduction...!

Since God has brought you into my life with a $58 Seed, it has turned my life around. God has changed my heart so much because of your wisdom and your ministry, I never knew God so personally as I am now learning about. I never knew how close to Him I could get and how much He could change things in my life and in me and in other people's lives just by believing that He could. I never knew what taking a step of faith could actually be and what it could do. I'm learning so much about the Lord that I never knew before.

He also took our back taxes from $75,000 to $5,729 from our $58 Seed.

J. & A. M. TN

My Child Can Walk...!

Thought I would write and let you know that my life is making severe changes. Sowing Seed into your ministry has brought about my first set of miracles. I have been sowing Seeds of $58 for over a year and a half to Daystar Television and I know that I have had several breakthroughs because of it. One of the $58 Seeds to the television ministry set a miracle in motion for my daughter… She was 2 1/2 and still not walking. I sowed, prayed and watched. She was in therapy because of her being premature. One of the therapists sat me down and told me she needed leg braces for at least a year and half before she would be able to walk. Within two weeks after their report, after the Seed, after the prayer she began to walk.

C. F. TX

Millionaire-Talk

MAN TALK

MIKE MURDOCK

31 Things You Will Need To Become A Millionaire

Man-Talk 20

DR. MIKE MURDOCK

31 Things You Will Need To Become A Millionaire (CD/MT-20)

MY GIFT OF APPRECIATION

GIFT of Appreciation

Wisdom Is The Principal Thing

Topics Include:

- ▶ *You Will Need Financial Heroes*
- ▶ *Your Willingness To Negotiate Everything*
- ▶ *You Must Have The Ability To Transfer Your Enthusiasm, Your Vision To Others*
- ▶ *Know Your Competition*
- ▶ *Be Willing To Train Your Team Personally As To Your Expectations*
- ▶ *Hire Professionals To Do A Professional's Job*

I have asked the Lord for 3,000 special partners who will sow an extra Seed of $58 towards the Ministry Outreaches. Your Seed is so appreciated! Remember to request this Gift CD, *31 Things You Will Need To Become A Millionaire,* when you write this week!

Miracle 7 BOOK PAK!

DREAM SEEDS
What Would You Attempt To Do If You Knew You Could Not Fail?
MIKE MURDOCK

VOLUME 17
SEEDS of WISDOM on FAVOR
MIKE MURDOCK
A Seven Day Mentorship Program Of Wisdom

SEEDS of WISDOM ON MIRACLES
VOLUME 1

SEEDS of WISDOM ON PRAYER
VOLUME 11

The JESUS BOOK
Everything The Father Wanted You To Know About His Son
MIKE MURDOCK

The Memory Bible on Miracles
MIKE MURDOCK

MIKE MURDOCK
The Mentor's Manna On Attitude
WISDOM SECRETS FROM THE HEART OF A M...

DR. MIKE MURDOCK

❶ **Dream Seeds**/<u>Book</u> (106pg/B-11/$9)

❷ **Seeds of Wisdom on Favor**/<u>Book</u> (32pg/B-119/$5)

❸ **Seeds of Wisdom on Miracles**/<u>Book</u> (32pg/B-15/$3)

❹ **Seeds of Wisdom on Prayer**/<u>Book</u> (32pg/B-23/$3)

❺ **The Jesus Book**/<u>Book</u> (166pg/B-27/$10)

❻ **The Memory Bible on Miracles**/<u>Book</u> (32pg/B-208/$3)

❼ **The Mentor's Manna on Attitude**/<u>Book</u> (32pg/B-58/$3)

**Each Wisdom Book may be purchased separately if so desired.

The Wisdom Center
Miracle 7 Book Pak!
Only $**30** ~~$36~~ Value
WBL-24
Wisdom Is The Principal Thing

Add 10% For S/H

Quantity Prices Available Upon Request

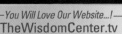

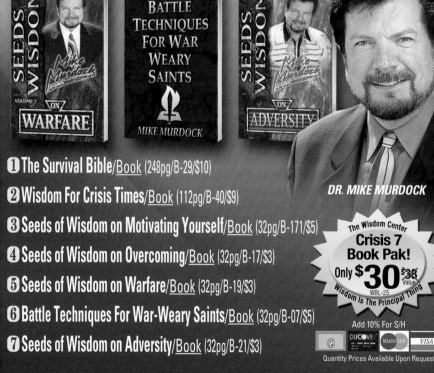

Career 7

Book Pak For Business People!

1. **The Businessman's Topical Bible**/<u>Book</u> (384pg/B-33/$10)

2. **31 Secrets for Career Success**/<u>Book</u> (114pg/B-44/$10)

3. **31 Scriptures Every Businessman Should Memorize**/<u>Book</u> (32pg/B-141/$3)

4. **Seeds of Wisdom on Goal-Setting**/<u>Book</u> (32pg/B-127/$5)

5. **Seeds of Wisdom on Problem-Solving**/<u>Book</u> (32pg/B-118/$5)

6. **Seeds of Wisdom on Productivity**/<u>Book</u> (32pg/B-137/$5)

7. **The Mentor's Manna on Achievement**/<u>Book</u> (32pg/B-79/$3)

**Each Wisdom Book may be purchased separately if so desired.

DR. MIKE MURDOCK

The Wisdom Center
Career 7 Book Pak!
Only $**30** $41 Value
WBL-27
Wisdom Is The Principal Thing

Add 10% For S/H

THE WISDOM CENTER 1-817-759-BOOK
4051 Denton Highway • Fort Worth, TX 76117   1-817-759-0300

You Will Love Our Website...!
TheWisdomCenter.tv   E

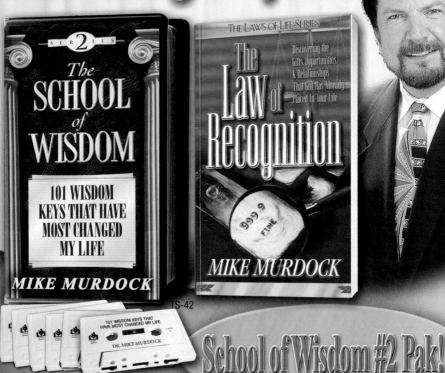

101 Wisdom Keys That Have Most Changed My Life.

THE LAWS OF LIFE SERIES

SERIES 2

The SCHOOL of WISDOM

101 WISDOM KEYS THAT HAVE MOST CHANGED MY LIFE

MIKE MURDOCK

The Law of Recognition

Discovering the Gifts, Opportunities, & Relationships That God Has Already Placed In Your Life

999.9 FINE

MIKE MURDOCK

TS-42

101 WISDOM KEYS THAT HAVE MOST CHANGED MY LIFE

DR. MIKE MURDOCK

School of Wisdom #2 Pak!

- ▶ What Attracts Others Toward You
- ▶ The Secret Of Multiplying Your Financial Blessings
- ▶ What Stops The Flow Of Your Faith
- ▶ Why Some Fail And Others Succeed
- ▶ How To Discern Your Life Assignment
- ▶ How To Create Currents Of Favor With Others
- ▶ How To Defeat Loneliness
- ▶ 47 Keys In Recognizing The Mate God Has Approved For You
- ▶ 14 Facts You Should Know About Your Gifts And Talents
- ▶ 17 Important Facts You Should Remember About Your Weakness
- ▶ And Much, Much More...

The Wisdom Center
School of Wisdom #2 Pak!
Only $30 $40 Value
PAK002
Wisdom Is The Principal Thing

Add 10% For S/H

DUCOVE   MasterCard   VISA

F

THE WISDOM CENTER
4051 Denton Highway • Fort Worth, TX 76117

1-817-759-BOOK
1-817-759-0300

You Will Love Our Website...!
TheWisdomCenter.tv

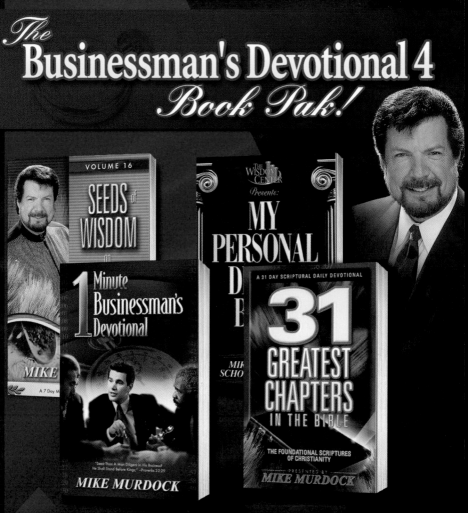

THE TURNAROUND Collection

① The Wisdom Commentary Vol. 1/<u>Book</u> (256pg/52 Topics/B-136/$20)

② Battle Techniques For War-Weary Saints/<u>Book</u> (32pg/B-07/$5)

③ Seeds of Wisdom on Overcoming/<u>Book</u> (32pg/B-17/$3)

④ The Memory Bible on Healing/<u>Book</u> (32pg/B-196/$3)

⑤ How To Turn Your Mistakes Into Miracles/<u>Book</u> (32pg/B-56/$5)

⑥ 7 Keys To Turning Your Life Around/<u>DVD</u> (MMPL-03D/$10)

⑦ The Sun Will Shine Again/<u>Music CD</u> (MMML-01/$10)

**Each Wisdom Product may be purchased separately if so desired.

The Wisdom Center
Celebrating 40 Years of Global Ministry!
Wisdom Is The Principal Thing

The Wisdom Center
The Turnaround Collection
Only $**40** $56 Value
PAK-15
Wisdom Is The Principal Thing

Add 10% For S/H

Favor 4!

This Collection Of Wisdom Will Change The Seasons Of Your Life Forever!

1 The School of Wisdom #4 / 31 Keys To Unleashing Uncommon Favor...Tape Series/6 Cassettes (TS-44/$30)

2 The Hidden Power Of Right Words... The Wisdom Center Pastoral Library/CD (WCPL-27/$10)

3 Seeds of Wisdom on Favor/Book (32pg/B-119/$5)

4 Seeds of Wisdom on Obedience/Book (32pg/B-20/$3)

**Each Wisdom Product may be purchased separately if so desired.

The Wisdom Center
Favor 4 Collection!
Only $35 $48 Value
PAK-12
Wisdom Is The Principal Thing

Add 10% For S/H

Financial $ecrets.

31 REASON$
PEOPLE DO NOT RECEIVE THEIR
FINANCIAL HARVE$T
THE 31 DAY MENTORSHIP PROGRAM
MIKE MURDOCK

VIDEO
7 KEYS to 1000 TIMES MORE
*The Lord God Of Your Fathers
Make You A Thousand Times
So Many More As You Are,
And Bless You, As He Hath
Promised You!*
Deuteronomy 1:11
MIKE MURDOCK

VI-16

Your Financial World Will Change Forever.

Video 2-Pak!

▸ 8 Scriptural Reasons You Should Pursue Financial Prosperity

▸ The Secret Prayer Key You Need When Making A Financial Request To God

▸ The Weapon Of Expectation And The 5 Miracles It Unlocks

▸ How To Discern Those Who Qualify To Receive Your Financial Assistance

▸ How To Predict The Miracle Moment God Will Schedule Your Financial Break through

▸ Habits Of Uncommon Achievers

▸ The Greatest Success Law I Ever Discovered

▸ How To Discern Your Place Of Assignment, The Only Place Financial Provision Is Guaranteed

▸ 3 Secret Keys In Solving Problems For Others

**Each Wisdom Product may be purchased separately if so desired.

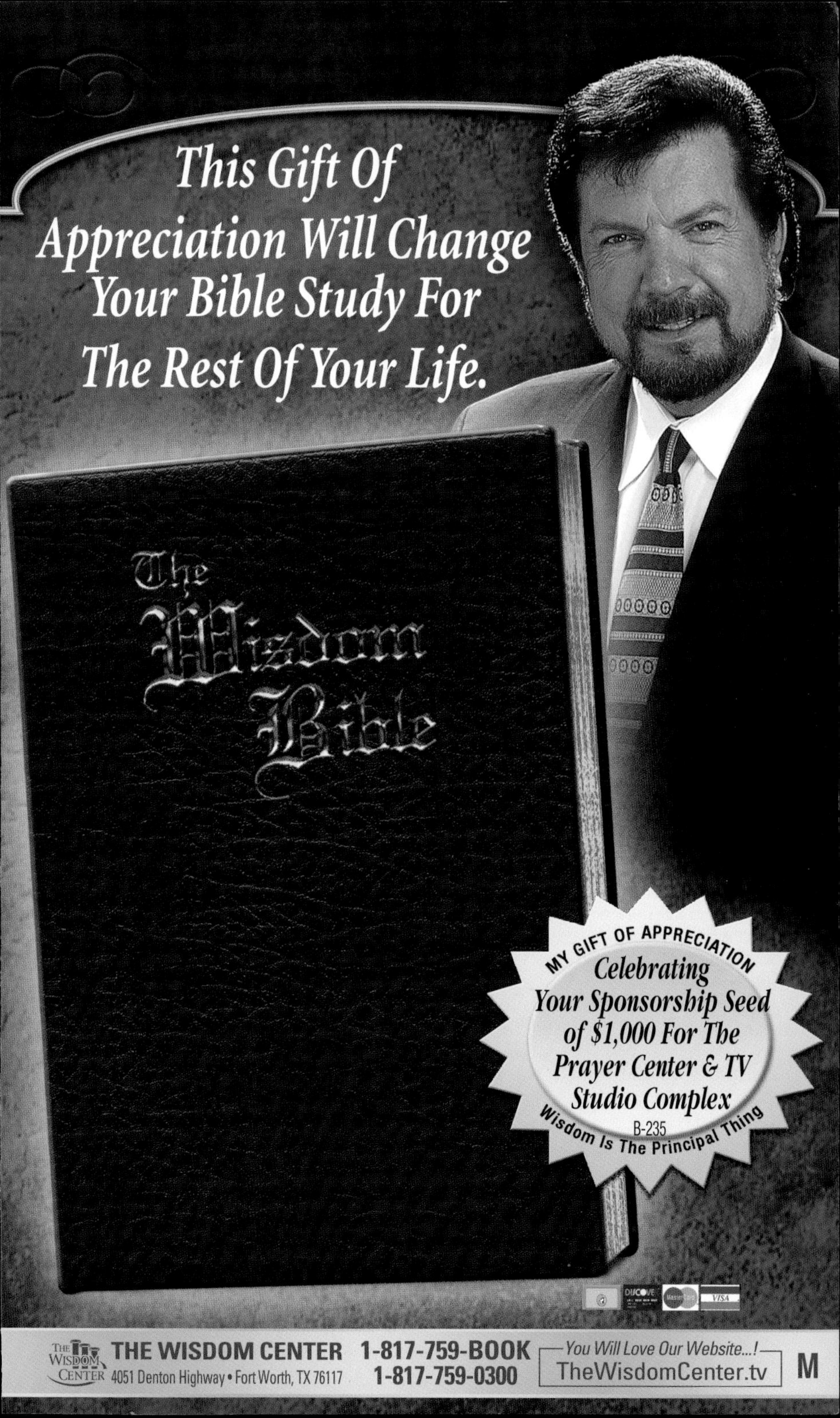
This Gift Of
Appreciation Will Change
Your Bible Study For
The Rest Of Your Life.
The Wisdom Bible
MY GIFT OF APPRECIATION
Celebrating
Your Sponsorship Seed
of $1,000 For The
Prayer Center & TV
Studio Complex
B-235
Wisdom Is The Principal Thing
THE WISDOM CENTER
THE WISDOM CENTER 1-817-759-BOOK
4051 Denton Highway • Fort Worth, TX 76117 1-817-759-0300
You Will Love Our Website...!
TheWisdomCenter.tv
M

Spirit Music.

The Mike Murdock Music Library

LOVE SONGS TO THE HOLY SPIRIT

Written In The Secret Place

TS-59

SERIES 1

LOVE SONGS TO THE HOLY SPIRIT

DR. MIKE MURDOCK

THE HOLY SPIRIT HANDBOOK

What You Need To Know About Your Daily Companion, The Holy Spirit

The Wisdom Center
Free Book ENCLOSED!
B-100 ($10 Value)
Wisdom Is The Principal Thing

Songs...

1. A Holy Place
2. Anything You Want
3. Everything Comes From You
4. Fill This Place With Your Presence
5. First Thing Every Morning
6. Holy Spirit, I Want To Hear You
7. Holy Spirit, Move Again
8. Holy Spirit, You Are Enough
9. I Don't Know What I Would Do Without You
10. I Let Go (Of Anything That Stops Me)
11. I'll Just Fall On You
12. I Love You, Holy Spirit
13. I'm Building My Life Around You
14. I'm Giving Myself To You
15. I'm In Love! I'm In Love!
16. I Need Water (Holy Spirit, You're My Well)
17. In The Secret Place

18. In Your Presence, I'm Always Changed
19. In Your Presence (Miracles Are Born)
20. I've Got To Live In Your Presence
21. I Want To Hear Your Voice
22. I Will Do Things Your Way
23. Just One Day At A Time
24. Meet Me In The Secret Place
25. More Than Ever Before
26. Nobody Else Does What You Do
27. No No Walls!
28. Nothing Else Matters Anymore (Since I've Been In The Presence Of You Lord)
29. Nowhere Else
30. Once Again You've Answered
31. Only A Fool Would Try (To Live Without You)
32. Take Me Now
33. Teach Me How To Please You

34. There's No Place I'd Rather Be
35. Thy Word Is All That Matters
36. When I Get In Your Presence
37. You're The Best Thing (That's Ever Happened To Me)
38. You Are Wonderful
39. You've Done It Once
40. You Keep Changing Me
41. You Satisfy

The Wisdom Center
6 Tapes / Only $30*
PAK007
Wisdom Is The Principal Thing

Add 10% For S/H

**Each Wisdom Product may be purchased separately if so desired.